Hank and I

A STORY OF COURAGE AND COMMITMENT,
FROM WWII HOLLAND TO A NEW LIFE IN AMERICA

CHRISTINA ROSMOLEN

Pleasant Word
A Division of WinePress Group

Pleasant Word (a division of WinePress Publishing, PO Box 428, Enumclaw, WA 98022) functions only as book publisher. As such, the ultimate design, content, editorial accuracy, and views expressed or implied in this work are those of the author.

Unless otherwise noted, all Scriptures are taken from the *Holy Bible, New International Version*®, *NIV*®. Copyright © 1973, 1978, 1984 by the International Bible Society. Used by permission of Zondervan. All rights reserved.

ISBN 13: 978-1-4141-1453-8
ISBN 10: 1-4141-1453-2
Library of Congress Catalog Card Number: 2009904057

TO MY CHILDREN

I want to tell you a story. It is a true story, about a boy and a girl who grew up in totally different environments in the Netherlands, and who fell in love toward the end of World War II. They merged their lives, like two streams flowing into a mighty river, and continued for sixty years, living most of these in the United States.

It is a story of adventure, great hardships, and great joys. It is the story of great love, burning like a bright flame till the end.

It is my story and his story, written down for you, our children, our children's children, and the future generations still to come.

PART I

One

VERY EARLY ON the morning of May 10, 1940, dawn broke softly through the mild darkness of the night over the city of Rotterdam, with the promise of another beautiful spring day. Something woke me out of a deep sleep. I didn't move, trying to recognize what had shocked me out of my dream. It was a noise, but what kind of noise? I heard it again, very real this time, and extremely loud. Explosions followed by heavy, droning sounds of planes flying overhead. Many planes and more explosions! A new sound joined in: sharp, short, staccato.

A vague fear gripped me. What was happening? Then I heard voices coming from the living room. Surprised that my grandparents and mother were up so early, I slid out of bed. I found them huddled in front of the small radio, listening intently to a male voice.

"What's going on?" I yawned.

The stunning answer came over the radio.

"We are at war!"

Confused, I grabbed a chair and sat down.

German troops had unexpectedly crossed the eastern borders of Holland, Belgium, and France early that morning! The newscaster was so excited that he stumbled over his words. The Nazis had rolled over the border with heavy armored tanks, accompanied by squadrons of planes in the sky.

Holland had stayed neutral during the First World War, and it was generally assumed that this war, too, would pass us by. Nevertheless, our troops were stationed at the eastern border because of the uneasy times. Germany had overrun Poland the previous September, after which England and France had declared war, but so far nothing much had happened. Until now. Our citizens were informed that our soldiers were putting up a fierce resistance and were engaged in heavy fighting. German planes were bombing strategic places all over our country, especially the harbor of Rotterdam. We stared at each other with unbelieving eyes while the explosions continued, sometimes accompanied by a sharp whistling noise as the bombs plunged toward the ground.

On this sunny spring morning in May, life as we knew it changed forever, never to return to its pre-war existence. Our world changed permanently, and the people with it. It was the end of a life that had simply been our life, familiar and mostly uneventful. The next five years would bring out the best or the worst in our people, depending upon individual character and attitude.

World War I, the war that was supposed to be the last one, had only spawned another one more terrible and more destructive, the beginning of a world in everlasting turmoil.

My life began in a dark and shabby apartment house in an old and narrow street in Rotterdam. A big, red-haired baby, I was born to an aloof mother and a father who sailed the oceans in a ship of the Holland America Line, and who was seldom home. I hardly knew my father, Christiaan, because he died off the coast of Rio de Janeiro when I was only two-and-a-half years old. He was only twenty-seven, and he died from a mysterious illness. My mother never knew the exact cause. We lived with my mother's parents. I don't remember hugs, kisses, love, or laughter from anyone. I only remember darkness and very little play.

Life existed mostly indoors. At about four or five years old I amused myself playing with buttons. They were my only toys. I liked my cigar box full of all kinds of buttons, and little as I was, I would make up all kinds of stories around them. The dark ones were boys. Light-colored ones were girls, and the big ones were fathers and mothers, aunts and uncles. I could be absorbed for hours playing with my button box.

In my uneventful life, however, Saturday nights were sometimes quite lively. Several uncles often joined my grandfather to play poker and drink beer. They settled in their shirtsleeves around the old dining room table, while the women were banished to the small living room. My cousin Corry and I would crouch in a corner, waiting for the fun to begin.

They were a loud, boisterous, opinionated group, these men. The card game always started out very pleasantly, even when they were playing for money, but very soon politics entered the conversation. In later years we learned about each man's political affiliation. Uncle Janus was a very noisy communist; Uncle Herman had joined the Dutch national socialist party, a forerunner of the Nazi party, and Thomas and Cor were die-hard socialists. Grandpa never admitted to anything. Before long, there would be lots of shouting, cursing, and pounding of fists.

When the arguing reached a high point, our small and feisty grandmother entered the room with a bundle of newspapers. Without any further comments the room quieted down, the cards were laid aside, and the table was covered with the newspapers. A big bowl was set in the middle. Grandmother entered again with a big bag of raw peanuts. Each man received a pile of peanuts in front of him, and without any protests they started shelling.

When the bowl was filled to the rim, it was taken to the tiny kitchen. We kids followed. Grandmother hauled out her enormous, black iron frying pan, having to lift it with two hands, and poured oil into it. The peanuts were dumped into sizzling oil, and she started to stir with a wooden spoon. The peanuts browned just right, not too pale, not too dark. Round and round went the spoon, and we soon smelled the delicious fragrance of frying peanuts. A generous dose of salt was added, and the golden nuts were poured back into the large bowl. Grandmother marched to the card players, and Corry and I were allowed to carry the little bowls and spoons.

The men sat peacefully around the table, smoking, and drinking another glass of beer. Bowls of hot nuts were passed around. The women took their portion to the living room. Corry and I found our spot in the corner again, with our full bowls on our laps. Crunch, crunch, it went around the table, and for a while all was peaceful and cozy.

After this traditional intermission the game would start up again, in a quiet, even polite manner. Soon someone would mention politics, and in no time at all the arguments were in full swing!

Grandfather, whom we called Opa, still worked at that time, operating one of the many cranes in the harbor, unloading cargo from the big ships that arrived from all over the world. Often Oma took his midday dinner to him and allowed me to go with her. She boiled potatoes and vegetables and scooped them into an enamel pot. On top went a piece of meat, and all was doused with thin, greasy gravy. Then she poured hot coffee into a gray enamel flask. Since we didn't live too far from the harbor, we walked there. We climbed the steps to the cubicle where Opa was busy turning all kinds of knobs, swinging large crates from a ship, and setting them down on the shore. I sat next to him for a little while and always received a bite from his warm dinner. It tasted better than the same food at home.

My grandparents knew poverty all their lives. Opa's parents turned him out of his home and family at age twelve because they could no longer afford to feed him. At this very young age he found work on the barges that carried freight on the Rhine River throughout Europe. A short, squat man with piercing brown eyes, he seldom smiled and possessed a dour disposition.

Oma was taken out of school at the age of eight and put to work as a maid, caring for young children. Her mother bore seventeen children, including four sets of twins. After the last one her father hanged himself, leaving the family destitute. An interesting legend was told about this family. Oma's grandmother, so the story went, was born a countess, living on an estate in the southern part of the province of Brabant. She fell in love with one of the farm hands and insisted on marrying him. Her father disowned her, and she left for a life of great poverty, which continued for generations.

Life proved so hard for my grandparents that they knew no joy, love, or optimism. Both of them grew up without any religion. They, as well as their children and extended family, did not believe in the existence of God. Jesus Christ was mentioned constantly, but always as a cuss word.

I also grew up without any knowledge of church, Sunday school, Bible stories, or prayer. If life was dark from my earliest recollections, the spiritual darkness was even deeper.

One of the many miracles governing my life was the certainty, buried deep within me, that my family lied to me. I was often told not to believe those stories about that Jewish carpenter, that they were all fairy-tales. Strangely, that did not change my certainty that there was a God. Young as I was, I had a clear picture in my mind of God. I saw Him as a kind old gentleman, with a long white beard, dressed in a long white robe, floating above me. I knew He was watching me, and my lonely little heart, starved for love, felt better when I thought about all that.

Where had I heard about God? Where did this belief come from? Who had whispered to me about Him? Many years later I realized that it was God Himself who had entered my heart and made me believe, and He walked beside me through all the turmoil and hardships still to come.

Two

 ⟶≋◯

WHEN I WAS five I acquired a stepfather, Gerard Appel, a hard man with pale, cold eyes and a bald head. From the day he met me he didn't like me, because I reminded him of my mother's first husband. Like my father before him, Gerard also sailed on a ship of the Holland America Line, as an electrician. He was gone a lot, too, and that became a great relief. Early in the marriage he engaged in enormous fights with my mother, causing great fear in me. The union was a mistake from the very beginning, but we were stuck with it. He swore and cussed constantly, and also proved to be violently against religion.

The plus side of all this was that we now lived in a nice ground-floor apartment on a decent street, close to a very nice school. A new little person entered my world: my sister Cora, five years younger than I.

I must tell more about this stepfather who entered so unexpectedly into my life. Over the years I learned that he came from a rather bad background. He was born in the Jordaan, which at the time was the worst slum in the city of Amsterdam. People living there spoke the most awful Dutch, hardly recognizable by other Amsterdam people. They were considered the class at the bottom of society. His father spent time in prison for sex crimes against children. His mother refused to acknowledge me because I was not Gerard's child.

Occasionally we traveled to Amsterdam by train to visit Gerard's parents, mostly around Christmas. We would always be served rabbit for dinner. Rabbit was a very popular holiday meat, like turkey in America. Gerard's mother would hang the rabbit, skin and all, in the bathroom to "ripen." When using the small, smelly bathroom, which we called the water closet, we would encounter the dead rabbit, emitting a dubious odor. After the rabbit was roasted, the company dinner was served. It tasted like it smelled.

I have often wondered how it was possible that Gerard had climbed up from the gutter he was born in, to being an electrician for the Holland America Line and later on Dutch oil tankers. Apparently, he was not dumb. Onboard ship he had picked up very respectable table manners, which he taught to us children. Much later, as a mature adult, and after I became a Christian, I started to understand how he could never have made a good and decent father, because he had never known one himself.

Besides being an atheist, he was also a communist, and was forever engaged in political arguments. He smoked constantly. His usual four packs of cigarettes a day were often not enough, and I was then sent to the corner tobacco shop to buy some more. A package of twenty "Pirates" cost ten cents in those days. All those many cigarettes were washed down constantly with black coffee, pot after pot. He did not die from lung or stomach cancer, or from a heart attack as might be expected. He died instead from gangrene in the leg in his seventies.

In the early 1930s the world plunged into a global depression, and Gerard was laid off from his seafaring job. He came home, and brought with him more unhappiness and more domestic fights.

His brother, Simon, also lost his job, and the two of them started a machine shop. They found repair work here and there, once installing equipment in a small laundry business somewhere in a village near Leiden, between Rotterdam and Amsterdam. It took a couple of weeks to install washing machines and dryers in those days because of all the electrical and plumbing work that was necessary. The owners, Hank and Maartje Rosmolen, were delighted with the job.

The Rosmolens were very religious. At one time they were Dutch Reformed, but after they came into contact with an itinerant evangelist who moved into their home for a while, they became convinced that the church did not preach the true freedom and religion in Christ. They quit going to church and began holding services at home. The Bible was read three times a day after each meal, concluded by long prayers. On Sundays the family sang hymns, accompanied on the organ by one of the daughters.

These simple country folks took an interest in Gerard and probably thought they could convert him. After the laundry job was finished, our family was invited to come and spend a weekend with them, just for pleasure.

And that is when I first met Hank, the youngest son.

I was eight years old at the time, and Hank was nine. Gerard had an old Ford for the business, and as we drove up to the house, leaving the car outside the gate, the first person who met us was this boy, Hank.

We stood there, staring at each other, not saying a word. I saw a real country boy, black stockings, three-quarter length pants, suspenders, and wooden shoes. In the city we didn't wear wooden shoes, and they fascinated me. He had very dark hair and greenish eyes, and a suntanned face, and he looked very solemn.

I was a city girl, with red hair and glasses, and I was wearing white kneesocks, a cotton dress, and plain shoes. At that time he was a little taller than I. Hank's mother invited us all in. We sat around the kitchen table with mugs of coffee, and milk for my little sister Cora, Hank, and me.

He kept looking at me, and after a while he said, "You want to play?" I nodded, and he actually took my hand and pulled me outside. As a total city girl, I had never been out in the country, and it opened up a new world to me. Hank showed me the garden, which was huge in my eyes. He took me to fruit trees, which had tiny apples hanging on the branches, informing me they were not yet ready to pick. He pointed out the last of the strawberries and picked one for me. Never had I eaten a strawberry from a real plant. I also had not known that apples grew on a tree or that milk came from a cow. He then took me to look at the neighbors' cows across the fence. They were bigger than I had imagined.

It became a day filled with new sights, and my love for the country was born in me right then. I was a big-city girl, but from that day on my heart belonged to the country.

On Sunday morning, Hank invited me to go with him in his canoe to the big lake at the end of the canal. I looked fearfully at the narrow little boat wobbling on the waves, and shook my head.

"I can't swim," I said.

"Not swim?" His eyes grew big. "But everybody can swim," he told me.

"Not me! And I won't go in that silly little boat!" I turned around and stalked off, fully expecting him to follow me. But he didn't. When I looked back, he was paddling away on the water, not paying me any more attention.

In spite of the disappointment that Hank left me, I had a great time those two days. I was enthralled by the house, which stood all by itself, meaning you could walk all around it. A real house surrounded by trees, flowers, chickens, ducks, and even a fat pig in a pen.

My mother, stepfather, and Hank's father talked a lot that weekend. Hank Senior did nothing but preach the gospel to them. Gerard pretended to accept it all and was quite agreeable to listen. The result of all this was that I was invited to come and spend the summer vacation with them, which in Holland was only the month of August. My mother accepted. So, instead of spending a whole summer month inside our apartment in a city street with nothing to do and no place to go, I would spend a whole month in the country!

That summer vacation became the best time I ever experienced. At nine years old Hank was expected to work in the garden. He helped by hoeing, weeding, bringing in vegetables, and even picking pears and apples. I happily helped him with his chores. On part of the property sat a large pile of fine gravel, and that was our favorite playground. We climbed to the top and slid down, becoming dirty and dusty, but we had great fun.

Hank had three sisters and a brother, all still at home. He was the youngest, his brother Bas was four years older, and the girls, Cor, Marie, and Pietertje, or "Pie," were around twenty. Cor, the oldest, was dating a young man by the name of Hannes Smits, who also lived with the Rosmolens.

Everybody worked in the laundry. The girls did all the actual work: sorting, marking, washing, drying, and ironing. They worked hard. Hannes picked up and delivered the loads. They had a *bakfiets*, which is a big cart, built on a three-wheel bicycle, to do the hauling. They had customers as far away as Leiden. All this work supported the family during the depression years. They also raised their own food and traded with their neighbors for milk and cheese.

That month with the Rosmolen family I wore wooden shoes, fed chickens, picked peaches and plums, and even acquired a healthy color. I slept in the attic, sharing a bed with Cor.

The only thing I found uncomfortable occurred in the evenings; when the weather was warm the outdoors beckoned, but we all had to come inside to read from the Bible out loud. The parents gave me a Bible, and I had to take part in the readings, too. It was all so strange to me, and besides, I had great trouble with the Old Dutch language in which it was written.

I hadn't thought about God since I was little, and I didn't understand about Jesus. I found those evenings difficult and boring, probably because I was only eight years old.

The summer vacation ended, and Hank and I did not see each other for the next five years. I was thirteen years old when we met again in 1938. The depression was nearing its end. My mother and Gerard had also started a laundry—a "self-laundry" it was called. We call it a laundromat now. Then it was an entirely new concept. It was a big place with washing machines where people could come and wash their clothes. A big contraption, called a *mangel*, ironed the clothes and sheets. Two people fed the sheets under this roll, and they would come out without a wrinkle, ready to fold. Later a small coffee shop was added. We lived above the business.

My mother and Gerard could not work together, and the fights became more violent. They seemed to really hate each other by then. When the screaming became too loud, neighbors on occasion called the police, to my deep and agonizing embarrassment. During that time a second sister was born, Anita. I was eleven years old then.

In the summer of 1938 the Rosmolen laundry needed some repairs, and Gerard and his brother spent a long weekend doing the job. When he returned I was told that I was invited again to spend a couple of weeks. I was in high school now and felt quite grown up at thirteen.

When I saw Hank again, I was shocked. I had grown a lot and was almost as tall as I would become, but he had not started to shoot up yet. He was fourteen now, and still a little boy as far as I was concerned. I thought he was a real country bumpkin, and he decided I was nothing but a stuck-up city slicker. That time he didn't pay much attention to me. There were relatives staying with them that summer, and he had more fun with uncles and cousins. Sister Cor had married Hannes, and sister Pietertje was dating Tony Van Gemeren. The laundry was busy, and that time I did not enjoy myself at all. Hank and I didn't play anymore; we were too old for that. I did get rides in his sailboat, though. Hank was a real water person, and he and his brother now owned a little sailboat. I was still afraid of the water and tried not to get into that boat too often. One of the best memories of that time was the food his mother cooked. I remember baked beans sweetened with beet syrup, salt pork simmered so it melted in your mouth, fantastic homemade brown bread, layered with homemade rhubarb jam. Aged cheese from the neighbors with the thick bread was a delicacy. Then there was an abundance of cherries, peaches, currants, gooseberries, and early apples, full of fragrant juice.

After this time at the Rosmolens our lives parted, and we would not see each other again until the winter of 1944, when I was nineteen and Hank was twenty.

Three

TOWARD THE END of the 1930s the economy started to improve, and Gerard went back to sea, this time on an oil tanker. The laundry was sold, and my mother and two sisters and I moved in again with my grandparents.

Life didn't change that much. There still did not exist any nurturing, or love, or warmth, or interest in children. The only thing different now was the lack of fights between our parents.

I went to high school, which I entered at age twelve. I was learning English, French, and German and soon learned to read simple stories in those languages. Because of my lonely, rather isolated childhood, I had become a voracious reader. I read everything I could lay my hands on. It had become an escape. I could separate myself from my real life and become immersed in the lives of the characters in my books. History books were my favorite, and then love stories, adventure, nature—anything. I have often wondered how I would have managed without reading.

I attended an all-girl high school, because my mother didn't believe in mixed education. She was fully convinced, and told me so, that I would go totally bad if I came into contact with boys. So I went to a school with 480 girls.

About the time I was in the second grade of high school, a teacher in the United States of America, in Lawrence, Kansas, came upon the idea that it would be a great thing if her pupils would write to children in other countries, to promote brotherhood. They would be allowed to choose the country. Three letters arrived in the office of the mayor of Rotterdam and were sent on to my school. All the girls had to draw a number to win one of the letters, and I was one of the lucky ones. It was written by a boy named Bob Moorman, who wanted to hear about wooden shoes and windmills. In my still very limited English, I wrote back and asked about cowboys, Indians, and movie stars. A correspondence started. His sister, Betty Jane, also started to write. We exchanged coins, like the small American dime, and the square Dutch nickel. It was exciting for me to have real American pen pals. Always a loner with few friends, I could boast now about friends in America! I became the envy of the kids at school! It was as good as reading my books.

Then, on that Friday morning in May 1940, when I had just turned fifteen, the war broke out! A new era, a new phase of life began. It all happened so quickly. Queen Wilhelmina fled to England. Princess Juliana and her family left for Canada. Our small army fought desperately for four days, trying to stem the tide of the Nazi hordes. The German government sent an ultimatum: surrender, or Rotterdam will be bombed! The order was ignored.

On Tuesday afternoon of May 14, a group of planes flew over the heart of the centuries-old city and dropped their lethal loads. First they bombed the waterworks and then, quite leisurely, destroyed the center of the beautiful city, which was founded in the year 800. It didn't take them very long, and after they disappeared over the horizon, they left behind a heaping, smoking mountain of rubble. The only building left standing was a movie house, owned by Germans. Our famous zoo was bombed, and for weeks afterward wild animals roamed the suburbs. Along one of the canals, storks had built their nests, but after the trees were destroyed they never returned. Traced to Egypt, where they flew in late fall, they had been a familiar sight each spring for decades.

Holland officially capitulated, and on May 15 we woke up under Nazi rule. The population gathered silently along the main roads leading into the city, watching tanks rolling by. Soldiers were sitting on top of them, laughing and eating, conquerors of a land, and heroes of the surprise attack on an unsuspecting population. Hatred was born.

At first we thought life had stopped forever, but it continued. Schools opened again. It was strange those first weeks, going to school and hearing the heavy sound of planes overhead, and meeting German soldiers marching in the streets. Very quickly we became aware of changes. Our schoolbooks had to be turned in, and were returned with holes cut into the pages, or black stripes blotting out any references to Jews, no matter how famous.

New laws affected the Jews almost immediately. They had to wear a large yellow star on all their items of clothing. It read, "Jood," the Dutch word for Jew. Even babies had to wear these disgusting patches. Next, the Jews could no longer ride the streetcars, or go to theaters, or shop outside of designated hours.

Every Dutch citizen received identification papers with their pictures, plus we now had ration cards. Some food items became scarce almost right away. The German armies, as well as their people back home, had to eat and the food was stolen from the occupied countries. Long, fully loaded freight trains passed through the country toward Germany, and gradually there was less and less for us. Long lines began to appear in front of stores for the inadequate supplies.

We also learned how dead bodies smelled. After the bombardment of Rotterdam, the Dutch estimate was thirty thousand casualties. The official German report was six hundred. When the cleanup began and the rubble was cleared, the bricks were piled up on a piece of land on the outskirts of the city. They were kept for the time when rebuilding would start. The odor of dead bodies clung to the porous bricks, and the summer turned quite hot that year. We could detect this sickening smell from a long distance away.

We were not done with bombs yet. The Allies started to bomb the large oil refineries of the Royal Dutch Shell and Texaco, which were located along the Rotterdam harbor. In the beginning they mostly bombed at night, under cover of darkness. Quite often the bombs would miss their target and fall on residential areas. The city didn't have bomb shelters and no places to hide for safety. Our family usually ran downstairs to the ground floor and huddled behind the front door, thinking that in case the house was hit, we could still get out into the street.

Fear became our constant companion, fear of being hit and killed by a bomb, fear of Germans, and fear of not having enough to eat. I remember my grandparents, my mother, sisters, and I all sitting around the table in the evening, listening. We were always listening. When the sirens started their shrill wailing, we sat up straighter and looked at each other with scared eyes. Soon the droning of the planes followed, many of them on their way to Germany. Furious anti-aircraft guns would start up. Some were mounted on trucks, which drove through the streets, inviting attacks from the planes. The harbor always got its share of bombs. We learned the particular whistling sounds of bombs falling very close. We held our breath, waiting to be hit, and then, when the explosion followed, we breathed again. It had hit somewhere else!

I had one good friend. Her name was Fietje. She was half Jewish and did not wear the hated yellow star. The Nazis had a theory: you could never doubt who someone's mother was, but the father was questionable. Therefore, Fietje, with a non-Jewish mother and a Jewish father, was relatively safe from being picked up on the street for being Jewish.

We became friends in high school, when we were thirteen. When I first met her she startled me with her homeliness. She was really ugly. Her features were all crooked, nose, mouth, with grown-together eyebrows. Therefore my first thought was, "What an ugly girl!" Until I got to know her. Her eyes were the loveliest, velvety, dark brown. Her smile, however crooked, showed perfect teeth; and her personality, all love and sweetness, wiped out the looks. Very soon you only noticed friendliness, warmth, and love, and Fietje became beautiful. She became my friend and introduced me to a different world. Her parents were wealthy, and she lived in a marvelous two-story house in an upscale neighborhood, with a maid, and a cook. I was invited to dinner sometimes, and that too was an eye opener.

The family gathered around a beautifully set table with wonderful food, like *real* meat roasted to perfection. Her mother was a lady and very friendly. Unfortunately, life didn't stay like that for them. Because of the Jewish father, a prominent businessman, the family appeared to be closely watched. Fietje's mother had relatives who had joined the Nazi party, and on order of the Germans they moved in with the family.

That, of course, became a tense and unhappy situation. Fietje's parents felt like prisoners in their own home.

Jews started to disappear, as well as other undesirable Dutchmen. One Friday afternoon, on the eve of the Jewish Sabbath, a girl in our class was hauled off during school hours by two burly German soldiers carrying big guns. She was never seen again. One of our most beloved teachers was also taken away, together with her bedridden old mother. I used to do their shopping for them because they were allowed only one hour per day to go to a store.

Life got scarier. And we became hungrier. Not as bad yet as it would become later in the war, but food was strictly rationed. Many items, which were ordinary staples, were gone. Oranges, bananas, coffee, and tea, always taken for granted, disappeared because they were imported. We drank surrogate coffee and tea, which tasted awful! Cream disappeared from the milk, which turned watery. Bread was rationed. At mealtime our portions were now carefully meted out, and they were not always enough.

On top of all that, the bombardments never ceased. There were rumors that the Germans were going to invade England, and the Rotterdam harbor was full of boats, large and small. The harbor was bombed almost daily, and several times apartment houses in our neighborhood were also destroyed, killing the people inside.

In the summer of 1941, I graduated from high school, at sixteen. My grandparents and mother decided then that we should move to the country, away from Rotterdam. Oma still had family in a small village in the province of Noord Brabant, in the southern part of Holland. They knew of a little house we could rent.

My stepfather, on an oil tanker, didn't come home any longer, of course. All Dutch oil tankers were in service of the Allies. Because he was now considered an enemy of the state, the Germans cut off my mother from any income. Soon after that, we received a visit from a stranger who informed my mother that he was part of a secret organization that provided income to people whose husbands were away working for the Allies. We started to receive a small income for the duration of the war. My grandparents received a small state pension, and with our combined finances we felt we could move to the country.

Four

SOON WE WERE settled in the village of Moerdijk, near the river Waal, which flowed into the Rhine farther down its course. The apartment in Rotterdam was kept, and Oma and Opa would pay the rent.

Life changed again. From a drab tenement house, we now lived in an old picturesque little house. A pump in the kitchen provided cold water, and a rickety outhouse nestled near the back door. Downstairs the kitchen was built into a corner of the small living room, next to a bedroom. A steep staircase led upstairs to one single bedroom, shared by my mother and me and Cora and Anita. Our only heat was a potbellied stove in the living area.

At first it was exciting and new to live in the country. Often we walked on the dike alongside the river and sat in the grass, looking out over the wide expanse of water, without being afraid of planes bombing us. We sometimes saw Oma's relatives, especially her sister, who lived with her son and his family.

Winter came very early that year, bringing with it harsh temperatures and much snow. The dilapidated outhouse was a horror to visit, especially on bitterly cold nights. The water in the pump sometimes froze, and by now food had become scarcer and scarcer. We still ate, however. Our relatives had a huge garden and brought us potatoes and large carrots, and occasionally a cabbage. They had a fruit cellar under their house, where they kept the food. They seemed not too happy to share, but for Oma's sake they did.

Soon I became bored. I could not just sit home in our cramped quarters and do nothing. A convent stood in the middle of the village. The Catholic nuns operated a day school for the local children. Cora and Anita enrolled in the village school, while I started at the convent, taking classes in sewing, pattern making, cooking, and general housework. With that we got a Catholic education, and had to join in prayers several times a day. I didn't think about God any longer in these bad times, but I had nothing against learning Catholic prayers and receiving Bible instruction.

One of the younger nuns also taught shorthand and typing. I eagerly added that to my lessons. I learned to type on the old manual typewriters, which by now are ancient antiques. I could type very fast, and I loved it. I also learned shorthand. I felt I might need that too, in the future, after the war was over, and I could get a decent job.

We were fed at the convent too. At noon we received a small hot meal, with one slice of homemade bread and a cup of milk. That was a wonderful bonus.

During that winter of 1942, I froze my toes. The snow fell thick and often, and I had no shoes. The last pair finally needed to be abandoned, and I made do with two wooden soles, like little planks, held to my feet with rope. A pair of my grandfather's woolen socks did nothing to keep me dry. My toes, especially the little ones, became severely frostbitten, and they turned a ghastly color and swelled alarmingly. They cracked open like an overripe plum, and the pain was unbearable. It became quite a horrible winter: never having enough to eat, always being cold, and the sore feet.

In the spring I had shoes again, secondhand from a dealer in worn goods. The pressure on top of my overly tender toes was hard to tolerate; besides, they didn't fit too well, but I had no choice.

One important thing I learned through all that: don't complain! Don't ever feel sorry for yourself. It can't be helped, anyway, and only makes other people feel bad, while you become more miserable. And things can always be worse. My basic nature must have been blessed with optimism, because I always saw a tiny ray of sunshine somewhere in the black clouds. I bore my sore toes in silence. During the following

years they became bent, deformed, and ugly, having taken a long time
to heal. But at least I still had all ten of them.

That icy winter of walking on my wooden planks has never faded
from my memory.

In early 1943, in the middle of the raging war, while I was living
in Moerdijk, Hank, now nineteen years old, still lived with his parents
in the village of Woubrugge. He helped to run the laundry, and hauled
and delivered clothes on the bicycle cart. He had also joined the local
resistance group, together with his brother Bas. By that time the Germans
were picking up young men from the occupied countries and sending
them to Germany to work in the war plants. So far, Hank had not yet
received the summons to report for work in Germany.

From early childhood on, Hank was a devout Christian. Raised
by his parents to believe in his Savior, the Lord Jesus Christ, he never
doubted his training, and as he explained later, Jesus became his constant
companion and greatest friend. In his teens he often wished the Lord
would use him to spread His words to others. He prayed for a chance
to be sent to people who didn't know Jesus.

One of his most-often told stories happened one evening when
he and his friend Jan came back from a neighboring village on their
bicycles. The path along the canal was narrow, and from the opposite
direction came three German soldiers, also on bikes. They all tried to
pass each other, and somehow Hank's front wheel struck a wheel of
one of the Germans, and they both crashed to the ground. One of the
others, obviously the leader, grabbed Hank as he got back on his feet,
and pointed his gun at him. Jan got scared, and he turned around and
hurried back in the direction from which they had come. The German,
with a threatening glare, poked Hank with his gun and said in halting
Dutch that he would be sent to a concentration camp for assaulting a
German soldier. Hank was just the right age to be sent to Germany to
work in the factories.

Hank stared back at the man and silently prayed.

"Lord," he said, "I have been asking you to send me somewhere so I can preach Your word to those who don't know You. If this is Your way that I should go to a concentration camp, then I accept this. Your will be done."

He became very calm, and waited. He thought about his mother and felt sorry for her, because of what would happen to him now. At that point the German dropped his gun, turned away, and without another word or glance the three soldiers got back on their bikes and continued on their way. Hank stared after them, disbelieving.

Having watched from a safe distance, Jan came back and asked, "What happened? Why did they back off?"

Hank shrugged. "I don't know."

Immediately he felt deep remorse. For the rest of his life he regretted that he didn't say to his friend, "The Lord rescued me."

He never forgot this incident, and many years later as he lay dying, he told this story to his pastor with tears in his eyes. The story went with him to heaven.

Shortly after that incident Hank got the summons to report for work in Germany. He pretended he was leaving, packed a suitcase, and said his good-byes. Even his mother didn't know he had other plans. He rode on his bicycle to his sister Cor, who now lived on an isolated farm in the country many miles away from his home. The Germans soon came around and asked his father why his son had not obeyed the work summons. His mother informed them that Hank had left for Germany. His father, in on the scheme, became very angry and shouted, "What have you done with my son?" The soldiers looked suspicious but could do nothing but leave.

Hank stayed away a year and worked the land with his brother-in-law until the early fall of 1944. His life was much more dangerous than mine. During the year he spent at his sister's home, he avoided many raids on young men. The Germans did not want young and able-bodied men to stay in Holland. The main reason was because they needed the men to be fighters in case of an Allied invasion against the Germans. The second reason was that they needed workers for the munitions factories in Germany. Somehow, the young men hiding among the farmers in this isolated area always received warning ahead of the raids.

Cor and Hannes lived in an old farmhouse with a cellar beneath the kitchen. This cellar had about a foot of water standing in it. It was sealed with a small trapdoor, which in turn was covered by linoleum and a table with four chairs. At the slightest hint of danger the table would quickly be put aside, the linoleum lifted, trap door opened, and Hank had to disappear into its blackness. Sometimes he stayed for hours in the bad-smelling water until the coast was clear. That is the spot where he spent his twentieth birthday.

By then he had had enough of that hidden life, so he returned to pick up his resistance activities again. The Resistance movement, or "Underground," as it was called, was very well organized. The men involved in it had weapons now. Allied planes would drop tommy guns and grenades into the countryside at night, after notifying the Dutch by secret radio of their coming. The Underground members took their bicycles to the appointed field, turned them upside down in a large circle and spun the wheels while shining flashlights on the wheel spokes, creating a ring of flickering light the Allied pilots could see. The planes would come in very low and drop their crates of weapons. The guns and ammunition were kept at different farms in the neighborhood. Hank's home was one of the places where the weapons were kept, without the knowledge of the other members of the family. Of course, the Germans were aware of the drops, and were always trying to find out who found them and where they were being kept.

Some of the Dutch, filled with hatred toward the enemy, took full revenge on the soldiers, often ambushing them in the dark. Hank and his brother Bas, being Christians raised in a Christian home, were more involved with aiding Allied pilots who were shot down.

Many times Allied planes roared over Holland on their way to Germany on bombing missions. Often they flew over the lake close to the Rosmolen home. The house would vibrate from the sound coming from the huge engines. Anti-aircraft guns located at Schiphol airport would swing into action, intent upon shooting down the planes before they reached Germany. Sometimes a plane would crash into the lake. Fast little motorboats of the Underground were ready, and before the Germans had a chance to pick up the surviving pilots, the villagers had fished them out of the water and taken them to designated farms.

One night a plane was shot down in a field near Hank's home, and miraculously the pilot, an American, got out before it blew up in towering flames. Hank and the members of the Underground had been waiting at the edge of the field. Before the Germans arrived, they hustled him to a farm. In the hay barn, they had constructed a hiding place in the middle of packed-in hay bales. Within the bales waited a tiny room furnished with a cot, a few blankets, and a pipe leading up to create an air vent. The American pilot was shown inside and the front bales were returned to their former position, and the young men returned home in the dark, satisfied that they had cheated the Germans out of another prisoner. Many years later Hank would find out what happened to that American pilot.

The pilots always wanted to get back to England, where they were greatly needed. Secret messages would come over hidden radios, and at the appointed time a submarine would lie in wait in the North Sea. On a dark night the pilots would be taken to the submarine in little rubber boats, safely delivered back into Allied hands.

Downed pilots had to eat, and food was scarce, even in the country. Any cattle, pigs, or sheep that were in the open were all taken to Germany. German trucks full of sheep sometimes passed through the village on their way to the border. Sheep had to eat, too, and sometimes they were let out in a particular pasture to graze. That is when Hank and Bas became expert sheep thieves. After curfew they would sneak out of the house at night intent on stealing a couple of fat sheep. They would trip them and then throw them into a water-filled ditch. When the way was clear, they would hoist the sheep on their shoulders and carry them home to be butchered. The meat was distributed first to the family and then to the hidden pilots.

The German garrison at Woubrugge consisted mostly of older soldiers. As the end of the war was getting closer, these men knew they were losing and were tired of the fighting. Interestingly enough, they were no longer willing to fight with the Underground. They were fully aware that the young men of the village were shooting off tommy guns at night in order to practice, but decided to ignore them. They did not want to be killed and had no desire to do any further killing themselves.

Five

MY MOTHER, EVER restless, didn't like living in the little house in Moerdijk any longer. She insisted on moving. With luck she found a larger house, two stories even, across from the small railroad station a couple of miles away. The rent was not very much, and it indeed appeared to be an improvement. The house had running cold water, and even a toilet inside. Oma and Opa moved with us, of course.

From the convent secretarial class I received a diploma in shorthand and typing, and I could now look for a real job. An insurance company in Dordrecht, across the water, hired me promptly. A long bridge connected the two sides of the river, and I started to commute by train every day. I worked five days a week, plus Saturdays till noon. Some businesses were still functioning in the Netherlands, and insurance was one of them. There were many restrictions, but some people were still working and earning an income.

Food, however, became more and more scarce, and some items had totally disappeared. Butter had long since disappeared, as well as meat, cheese, and eggs. Anything imported had become a memory. We could only buy food with our coupons, and that meant very little.

In the fall of 1943, barely eighteen, I became a smuggler. Our income, provided by the secret seamen's organization, was small, and my twenty-five guilders a week were very helpful, but not adequate.

By that time our family had become friendly with a Dutch policeman by the name of Koen. Koen was a loyal Dutchman, and he despised the Nazis. One day he approached me and asked if I would be willing to smuggle wheat into Dordrecht and sell it on the black market. He could get raw wheat in Belgium, smuggle it across the border, divide it into five-pound bags, and then bring it to me. I could then sell it for him in the city and make a small profit, and was also allowed to keep some wheat for my family. That was black marketeering, of course, and when caught you were in deep trouble. People liked raw wheat. They ground it up in their coffee grinders and then you could cook it in water, like a hot cereal, or make pancakes with it, or even bread, if you were lucky enough to have yeast and an oven.

It was a dangerous game. When caught smuggling, you were taking food away from the German population, and punishment was severe. I considered it seriously. I would get free wheat for my family and earn much needed money.

So my smuggling career started. I was not afraid. By that time I had become rather numb toward all the hardships and the fear. I just did what had to be done in order to survive. I was considered the head of the household and carried the responsibilities that a father would carry. They all depended on me. My teenage years were slipping away into nothing. Fun did not exist. We always stayed home, depressed, hungry, in a sad atmosphere. My mother could not cope very well with the circumstances and complained steadily. Life rolled on one day at a time.

The smuggling was a matter of survival for the family. Every morning, catching the train across the river I carried a school bag with five pounds of wheat. I looked very young at eighteen, exactly like a schoolgirl. A noisy group of boys were always on the train, having come from the city of Breda and going to a technical school in Dordrecht. They were about my age and younger, and always occupied a compartment in the last car. I decided they would be my cover. Every morning I entered their compartment, threw my wheat-stuffed bag in the overhead net, and sat down among them. I was not popular. I knew they thought I was a pushy girl who had no business being there. They mostly gave me dirty looks and then ignored me.

In spite of the unfriendly atmosphere, I felt safe with them, safer than with adult passengers who often were searched. Whenever the occupants of the train were being checked, German soldiers would open the compartment door, take one look at the noisy young crowd, and slam the door shut again.

When the train pulled out of the station, I sighed with relief and suffered the twenty-minute ride into Dordrecht. There awaited the next tricky situation. I had to pass through the gate where very often Germans would stand, stopping people and searching their luggage. Whenever I spotted them I would walk closely with some boy, whether he liked it or not, and nonchalantly walk through the gate. I was never stopped during the entire year of my smuggling activities.

My black market business helped the family a lot, and often now we could fill our hungry stomachs with wheat cooked in water or with rather dry pancakes, which all tasted delicious to us.

My office work consisted of typing, taking dictations, and filing. It was not exactly a happy place. How could it be? We all lived under the same oppression and with fear of the Germans. I had no friends and no opportunity to make any. I commuted by train, and most of the other people lived right in town. During that time I received a short letter from Fietje's mother. I had been writing to Fietje after we left Rotterdam. Both Fietje and her sister Marianne had been picked up by the Germans early one morning. No one had heard from them since. And no one knew the reason. It came as a great shock! She was the first person I personally knew who had been arrested and hauled away. Shortly after that a young man at the office who, it was rumored, was aiding Jews, also was arrested. Later we found out that he was shot. It made me wonder sometimes how long I could keep up the smuggling. But I doggedly kept going. Having started, I felt I could not quit. People in the city were happy to pay for the wheat, I made a small profit, and my family ate a little better.

Another winter loomed. The evenings were spent at home, of course. There existed a curfew, and we had to be inside after dark.

One evening a scary thing happened. We were all huddled around the stove in the living room, where a sputtering fire tried to create some warmth. My old coat was wrapped around me, but I still shivered. No one was moving outside, so the sudden sound of the doorbell startled us. What now? Who could be out there on this dark night? That only meant trouble.

The doorbell rang again, this time accompanied by pounding. As the oldest, I warily got to my feet, dropped my coat, and slowly went to the front door. I paused a few seconds and then opened it. I looked straight into a skull, light shining through its empty eye sockets, and grinning open-mouthed. Inky blackness surrounded the thing, which kept staring at me. It seemed to just float in the air.

Too stunned to feel anything, even fear, I held myself very still, hardly breathing. The skull didn't move either. My muscles tensed and the seconds, or maybe minutes, passed. The obscene confrontation continued. Then, from somewhere behind the apparition I heard a suppressed giggle. I relaxed. It was a prank. Those pesky boys from across the alley, of course! They were waiting for my scream. Where did that skull come from? Was it real? How did they hold it up? Very slowly, without a sound, I closed the door. I leaned against the icy wall, breathing hard now and feeling weak. After a while I went back into the room and said, "It was nothing."

No one asked any questions. There was never any talk about this in the neighborhood. Everything went on as usual. After thinking it over, I found it rather funny, in spite of its being one of the scariest moments in a scary time.

During this time of hunger, fear, and depression, I never thought about God. The kind, loving presence that hovered over me in my early childhood was long forgotten. There simply was no room in my mind for love or kindness, least of all God. We lived in darkness, a great spiritual darkness, totally absorbed by the daily struggles of just living and staying alive. It occurred to me from time to time that God must not really exist, because if He did, He would not let all this misery happen. Religious life was so far removed from my life, there was no bridge between.

God, however, had not forgotten me! One day I missed the commuter train after work, which had never happened before. As I entered the platform, it had just left, leaving me standing there, staring after it. I could do nothing but wait. I sat down in the waiting room, very much aware of my hungry stomach. After what seemed to be an endless hour and a half, I finally got on the next train. It traveled unusually slowly across the river. When I finally arrived at the station across from my house, I noticed lots of commotion everywhere. My mother stood there looking wild and distraught. Lots of German soldiers filled the platform, some of them covered with blood. I saw bodies lying on the ground in a neat row.

The train I missed had been attacked by a plane that suddenly appeared from the clouds, shooting its guns at the windows. This particular train often transported troops, and the Allies must have known about it.

Why had I missed that train? I didn't have a reason. Why had I been saved from this attack? It puzzled me greatly for a while, but I soon forgot about it. Other events were happening.

Six

MY MOTHER DECIDED that living in the country was not really any safer than living in the city. Oma and Opa missed their little apartment in Rotterdam, so the three of them made a plan to move again, my grandparents back to Rotterdam and the rest of us to Amsterdam. My mother had become friends with a woman who also had a husband at sea, but he was captain of his ship, and they were quite wealthy. The two women had met early in the war at some seamen's wives' gathering. Marie lived in Amsterdam and assured my mother she would find us a place to live.

We found a second-story apartment alongside one of the old canals. It bordered on the area where many Jews lived. I had to quit my job in Dordrecht, but the worst aspect of this move was that I also lost my smuggling business. We would no longer have the much-needed extra money, and no wheat for us.

Right away I found another job, this time at the central office of the Dutch Beer Breweries. Beer was still being brewed, mostly for Germany, and this office was the central distributor of the grains required for production. The office was located in a very old picturesque building in the heart of Amsterdam, causing quite a long walk from our apartment. At the time I didn't know this, but every day I passed Anne Frank's hiding place. When the story of Anne Frank came out after the war and her diary was published, I realized this from the address of the house with the attic.

With the wheat smuggling over, food became a daily struggle. It was now the spring of 1944, and we were headed for the worst months yet to come. I was earning a much better salary and sometimes I could buy some food on the black market. I would come home with two eggs, a half loaf of sticky black bread, or a few potatoes.

By unspoken agreement my mother and I always gave the better food to my younger sisters because they needed it the most. If we had two eggs, we gave them to Cora and Anita. If miraculously we got hold of an orange, the girls ate the fruit and we ate the peel. One of the uncles, my mother's brother Cor, came to visit. He complained loudly that my sisters got the same amount of food as the grownups, even a bit more. To my utter amazement, my mother took him by the collar and literally threw him out of the door with great satisfaction. The best and finest thing about her was the total unselfishness with which she divided the food.

I was glad my stepfather was not around during those years. He would have been no help at all, and would have thought about his own needs first.

Often I thought about my own father. I knew so very little about him. From old pictures I could see that he was a very tall, slim, and handsome man, impressive in his uniform. I had heard stories mostly from my grandparents and uncles and aunts. They all liked him very much. His mother didn't want him to marry my mother, because she came from a lower class. He ignored her wishes and married anyway. He was promptly disowned by his family. After I was born he informed his father and mother that he now had a little daughter. The answer came that they still did not wish to have anything to do with his wife but, if he wanted, he could come and show the little girl. He never did.

My mother and he were married for five years. Most of that time he sailed all over the world, sometimes on freighters, sometimes on big passenger liners. When he reached twenty-seven, his ship was anchored off the coast of Rio de Janeiro and he became very ill. The ship's doctor gave him some pills and he died within a half hour. So the story went.

It was never clear what caused his death, and my mother never found out. It remained a mystery.

My father's older brother had died on his wedding night at twenty-four. The other brother never had any children. I remained the only grandchild. In spite of that, my father's family never contacted my mother to meet me or acknowledge me.

His name was Christiaan, and my name was the feminine version, Christina. I have always been glad to be named after him. At least there has always been that connection.

For years my mother kept a thick packet of his letters. One day when I was about ten she burned them all. The reason was that my stepfather had been snooping around and read them. I regret she didn't give them to me. It would have been my only link to him—to have his words, his thoughts, on paper to cherish for the rest of my life.

I knew with certainty that he had loved me very much until one day when I overheard my mother telling a friend, "Chris didn't like children. Not to kill them, but he didn't like them."

Those words devastated me! Always thinking at least one person in my life had loved me, that illusion was taken away from me now! Of course, it could have been a gross exaggeration, but it stung deeply. After that he became a shadowy figure retreating into the past.

In the spring of 1944, I became quite settled in my new job, even though I did not quite fit in. All the other girls working there came from a better social class than I did. In Holland at that time and long before, a very obvious and sharp distinction existed between classes. The daughter of a lawyer or doctor would never socialize with someone who came from the working or blue-collar class. I came from a poor family, my mother spoke "low" Dutch, and we lived in a rundown neighborhood in a shabby house. I was fully aware of my standing. However, I could type and take shorthand with the best of them. I often took dictation from the big boss feared by the others because he was such a bully. I was the only one who dared go into his office to take his dictation, which was fast and furious most of the time.

It surprised me enormously when one of the in-group approached me. She rarely spoke to me, but now she asked me if I would be willing to help deliver clandestine newsletters around my neighborhood. We were not allowed to have any radios. Early in the occupation all citizens had to hand over their radios so that we would not be able to listen to the BBC and hear the other side's news of what was happening with the war. We were allowed only German news in our newspapers, which was mostly lies. Of course, some people kept their radios and hid them, and some were even so brave as to write down the news, copy it, and spread it around.

Delivering these outlawed news pamphlets would be a tricky thing. It meant going out after dark, after curfew even, and slipping the papers into people's mail slots. In front of this girl I did not want to seem a coward, so I answered bravely, "Sure."

On the appointed evening I sneaked out of the apartment after my mother and sisters had gone to bed, and met the girl at the street corner. It surprised me that she really came. I didn't think that people from such good families would do things like that. I could barely see her in the dark. She held out a small bundle of papers and said, "You go around the block here, and I will take the next one, and we will meet here again. Be careful. If you are caught, I never saw you and don't know you."

Hesitantly I started out. My throat felt dry and my heart pounded. Why had I said that I would do this? It was crazy! If something went wrong, what would happen to my mother and sisters?

It went fine at first. I stayed close to the houses. There was enough light from a sliver of moon that I could make out the doors. Each door had a copper slot through which the mail was deposited. Becoming confident after the first few deliveries, I felt no fear any more. This was a good thing! All done for a patriotic cause! And right under the noses of the Germans.

Then it happened! Just as I inserted a paper into a slot, the door opened and a male voice exclaimed, "You there!"

I whirled around, rushed down the steps and started running along the canal, papers clamped tightly in my hand. To my horror, footsteps were following me.

A man hissed, "Stop!"

I was not much of a runner and could hardly get my breath. I knew he would catch me, and suddenly I gave up. I turned around, my back against a tree, and waited. So be it. I felt deeply sorry for my family because they needed me. What would happen to them?

The man stopped right in front of me.

"Are you the one who delivers those newsletters?" he growled.

Suddenly I was quite proud of myself and lifted my head high. I was ready to accept the consequences. "Yes!" I almost shouted.

"Hush," he answered. "I just wanted to ask you, can you deliver fifty more the next time?"

My career as an underground newsletter deliverer ended shortly after that. I did not regret it.

On June 6 of that year, after arriving at the office, I heard incredible news. The Allies had landed in France! No one was able to work. We all sat in little groups, repeating the rumors brought by someone who still owned a radio. After a while we all left without asking permission, laughing and joking and saying, "The end is here! The war will soon be over now!"

I ran home as quickly as I could and almost fell into the house. My mother listened wide-eyed when I told her the fabulous news. We so seldom heard good and uplifting news. And this, that the Americans, the British, the French, and other nations had invaded the continent and were going to get rid of Hitler and his cronies, was the desperately needed shot in the arm.

We had lived through four years of oppression and suffering and we were so naïve! The Dutch people fully expected the war to end now. We were so hungry for it. That day people started to gather on street corners, which according to German rule was strictly forbidden, but no one cared. People started telling each other that the Allied troops were already on their way to Amsterdam to liberate us.

Since then I have often wondered how people could really believe that. It was not logical. At the time we knew nothing about what was happening on the Normandy beaches, about the many lives being lost, and the heavy fighting that was going on. But to entertain the thought that the Allies had landed only to liberate Holland was strange indeed. The depression, the grieving, the fear, the hardships had gone so deep that the people grabbed at a thread to be lifted up and feel hope again.

In the late afternoon that June day, something happened. Amsterdam citizens started to arrive and stand on the bridges leading into the city. They carried bouquets of flowers. They waited for the liberators, who did not come. The day came to an end, and darkness started to color the sky. Heads drooped again and the people shuffled away, wilting flowers in their hands. The ray of hope had disappeared.

Nothing changed for us, except that we found out things could get much worse.

Seven

FURY POSSESSED THE Germans. The invasion hit them hard and they were more determined than ever to win the war. They hauled away Jews with more ferocity than ever before. They wanted to annihilate as many as possible. Old men, young men, old women, young women, children, babies; it did not matter. They were to be destroyed. Loaded freight trains jammed with Jews from all over Europe were constantly arriving at the brutal concentration camps in Poland and eastern Germany. After discharging the human cargos, they returned empty to fill them up again. We knew, of course, that the Jews were in camps, being treated badly, but we did not know that there was a massacre going on, that ten million people would be murdered and gassed by the end of the war.

In Holland, especially western Holland, food became so scarce now that sometimes we didn't have anything to eat for several days. It became harder and harder even to find food on the black market. We started to eat tulip bulbs, whenever I was lucky enough to be able to buy a few pounds. We became thinner and weaker and went to bed at six in the evening, sleeping around the clock or longer, because as my mother said, "When you are asleep you don't feel hunger."

Another winter approached and became known as the "Hunger Winter of 1944." Streetcars quit running. There was no heat, no electricity. Gas was available only one hour per day, in the evening. It became bitterly cold, inside as well as outside. Evenings we lived in the dark, with one small candle in the middle of the table. The feeble light did not allow any reading. We did not possess a radio, and entertainment belonged to the past.

Food became our number one thought. It possessed us. It dominated our waking hours. We dreamt about it. What could we find to eat? Where to find it? Whenever I got hold of some bulbs, we considered that a feast. My mother peeled them, sliced them, and cooked them with a little cabbage. Sometimes there was a little cabbage for sale, but not always. We were happy whenever we had bulbs to eat in the evening. At least we ate something hot, even if it consisted of a soupy mess, tasteless and a bit poisonous. After eating bulbs, quite often our skin developed sores that were hard to heal.

We had a little potbellied stove in our sitting room. Furniture became fuel. We took one chair at a time, sawed off an armrest or a leg, and burned that for a little warmth.

The soles of our shoes were totally worn through. Every morning I stuffed old newspapers in my shoes before I walked to work. When it rained or snowed the paper would disintegrate almost immediately, and the rest of the day I would suffer cold, wet feet. In the unheated office my feet would feel like blocks of ice. Amidst of all this I still went to work every day, because we needed a paycheck.

Living on the edge of the Jewish quarter, we often witnessed terrible happenings. Some nights big trucks pulled up, blocking the entrances into the area. Great searchlights illuminated the deserted streets. Uniformed men, mostly Gestapo, swarmed into the houses and soon brought out crying children, old people who could barely walk, men, and women. Some were in nightclothes. Like sheep they stood in line waiting to be thrown into the trucks. Some tried to escape and jumped into the canal. These poor brave souls were always shot, and their bodies floated until fished out of the water with meat hooks.

We sat in our room trembling with fear, hearing the shouting, crying, and screaming, along with the rough German voices, and we wondered when it would be our turn.

During this scary time a girl at the office offered me a free ticket to a concert at the Amsterdam Concert Gebouw. The conductor was quite famous, and I had never attended a concert at this revered place. The program was music by Edvard Grieg, a Norwegian composer.

On a dark Sunday afternoon I entered the big concert hall. To my surprise I saw a large crowd. The stone building was not heated, and only feeble light entered through slits in the wall. Shivering in my coat, I found my seat and noticed that everyone was covered by coats, hats, scarves, and even blankets. When the members of the orchestra entered the stage, they, too, wore coats. Many of them wore gloves without fingers.

The music took me into another world. They played "The Last Spring," and the melancholy sound penetrated the gloomy, icy-cold atmosphere like an affirmation of what life was all about outside the building. I felt transported into a world of sad beauty and great art. Forever after, Grieg's music became my favorite of the classics.

The concert ended. The musicians sat motionless on the stage, apparently waiting for applause. No one clapped. A deep quiet lingered in the aftermath of the glorious sound. Then, here and there, someone slowly stood. Soon everyone rose, still not applauding. Under a deadly silence the crowd shuffled out of the building, not speaking, not even coughing.

Out on the street everyone went their own way. I believe people were so downtrodden, so psychologically beaten, that it was difficult to express any kind of exuberance after being touched by such music. Or, perhaps the deep silence was the greatest tribute we could give to the musicians who had done their best to create a diversion from the circumstances. I never forgot that concert or the silence afterward.

In the middle of November my mother, restless as ever, suddenly decided she wanted to go see her parents in Rotterdam. Trains and buses were no longer running and I asked pointedly how she intended to get there. She had it all worked out. "We'll go with a barge. They are still going up and down to Rotterdam."

"But how will we get permission to go with a barge?" I shook my head.

She would not recognize the difficulty of her plan. "You go and find us a barge. I'm sure there will be someone willing to take us."

I was not as brave as I would have liked to be, or pretended to be. Everything scared me—the war, the persecutions, the hunger, the bombs, the shootings. Not being a rebellious person, however, I started out along the big canals and waterways of Amsterdam. Some barges seemed to be deserted, but sometimes people were working on deck. I stopped and talked to several men. They all looked at me as if I had lost my mind. Some didn't even answer me. Others just shook their heads and disappeared below deck to get rid of me. One skipper, a small, wiry man with sharp blue eyes, agreed to take us. It astonished me when he nodded and asked, "When do you want to go?"

"Whenever it is okay with you," I answered. It was highly against the rules to take unauthorized passengers, but he seemed to enjoy putting one over on the Germans. He did set rules—we had to be at the boat at daybreak, and we had to be hidden when necessary. If the Germans would come to inspect the boat and find us, it would mean trouble for us all. Most amazing of all was that he didn't want any payment for this journey.

A few days later, as soon as curfew was lifted, my mother, Cora, Anita, and I set out for the canal near the harbor. It was a drizzly cold morning, but we were dressed as warmly as possible. All four of us had eaten a piece of the soggy brown bread that was our allotment for the week. Anita, the youngest, even had some milk. Each week children were allowed one pint of the watery substance with a hint of white in it.

We found the barge. The gruff skipper let us climb down into it, turning his head in all directions to see if we were being watched. His cabin smelled oily and dusty. He pointed at a narrow door in the corner.

"That is your hiding place. When we get a German patrol, get in there quickly, and don't you dare make a noise. Hide behind the clothes."

Soon the engine started to throb, and the barge slowly slid away from its mooring place. The four of us huddled closely together on the bench, trying to get some warmth from each other.

Some time during the day the skipper came down the short steps and took a paper bag out of a cupboard. He sat down at the small table and unwrapped a large slice of thick brown bread covered with a slice of yellow cheese. He unscrewed a thermos bottle, and the smell of hot coffee invaded the cabin. Even today, after sixty-five years I can see him eating his meal, oblivious to our family watching him. We were starving, and tears filled my eyes for my sisters, whose skinny bodies were pressed into mine. They watched him silently with yearning eyes.

The skipper went on deck again, and we just sat there, occasionally using the little privy in a tiny closet. In late afternoon the barge stopped. We heard loud voices and stamping of feet. The man came down and said, "Quick! The German patrol is on board. Get in the closet!" He opened the narrow door.

My mother started to cry, and whimpered, "Christina, you go in front. Then they will get you first."

She crawled into the closet first, then in went my sisters, and I stood in front. The closet was very low. We crouched and could hardly breathe. The air was sticky and oily from dirty clothes hanging in there.

Heavy footsteps sounded overhead. Men entered the cabin. We heard laughter and German words. No one seemed to be in a hurry. The air became thick and breathing became labored. After what seemed an eternity the patrol left and the barge started to move again.

We were then allowed to come on deck, and we filled our lungs with delicious cold, fresh air. We had not eaten since our meager breakfast. I ached for my sisters, and felt their pain and empty stomachs even worse than my own. I could not help them. I thought this whole scheme of my mother wanting to go and visit her parents in these difficult times was ridiculous. Oma and Opa would not have enough to eat, either, and we would just be a burden to them.

It was getting late, and would be dark soon. We sat flat on the deck in the back when a new danger threatened. The Germans had been shooting off a new weapon, a rocket like a flying bomb. These were launched from different locations in western Holland. They would rise into the sky and then head west toward England. Sometimes the rocket, called a V-1, would malfunction and fall back to the ground, causing considerable damage and even killing people.

To our horror we saw a rocket rise into the sky, rather close. As we stared, it sputtered, halted, and returned to earth with a screeching noise. It splashed into the water, throwing up a mighty fountain amidst a loud explosion. Quite shaken, we went back to the musty cabin where we dozed the night away, half sitting and half lying. The skipper didn't come down. Apparently he had permission to keep on going through the night.

Very early the next morning we arrived in Rotterdam in a quiet part of the harbor. It was cold and misty. After thanking the dour skipper, we hurried off the boat. Oma and Opa did not live too far away, in the familiar old district near the harbor. It was the place from which we had fled a couple of years earlier to go and live in the country.

When we turned the corner into Harper Street and searched out the house, we saw Oma standing behind the second-story window watching for us. It was so good to see them again, to be with family once more. They looked so small, old, and skinny!

A little fire in the round stove tried to warm the living room. Opa was busy in the tiny kitchen, frying pancakes on an oil burner. They smelled heavenly, and I felt my stomach cramping for the lack of food. The pancakes were a mixture of oatmeal and ground wheat with water. Opa must have gotten hold of some fat, because the dough sizzled as he poured it into the pan. We devoured the pancakes hot and dry. It was the first food we had tasted in quite a while, and it was the best we had ever eaten, we said. Opa explained that Uncle Thomas, one of my mother's brothers, brought them extra food from time to time. He was a policeman on the river, the "water police" they were called. Sometimes he would get food from smugglers if he closed an eye to their illegal activities. He always brought some of the food to his parents. I was so glad to hear that my grandparents were not totally starving like so many of the Dutch people.

We spent a couple of days with them. We rarely ventured out onto the street. We endured the bomb attacks, which occurred almost daily. The evenings were spent sitting in the living room around the table with a candle in the middle, just like at home. Uncle Thomas came to visit a couple of times. Once he brought a sack of potatoes. Oma boiled them and we each got one. With a bit of cabbage added on our plates, we had a feast.

On the fifth day my mother wished to go home again to Amsterdam. She had it all figured out. She approached me one morning and said, "I think we should go back, but try to get a permit from the Germans."

I was stunned. "And how are we supposed to get such a permit?" I wanted to know.

"That's simple. Just go to German headquarters and ask for one."

"The German headquarters?" I couldn't believe my ears.

She became impatient. "Just go there, and get a permit."

German headquarters was located somewhere downtown, on the edge of the bombed-out center. I vaguely remembered that. She handed me my coat and almost pushed me out of the door. I stood on the bleak, quiet street, shivering in the rain. Going to the Germans scared me. I had lived too long with so much fear, and now I had to go and ask favors from the enemy.

I started walking. There were people about, pale, skinny, and walking with bent heads, dressed in ragged clothes. Very occasionally I saw a Jew with the bright yellow star on a threadbare coat. I was amazed that they had the courage to venture outside, and was even more surprised that there were still Jews left.

Headquarters was a busy place, uniforms everywhere. A giant photo of Hitler hung in the hall and there were flags with swastikas everywhere. A fat, round-faced woman in a tight uniform was seated at a desk. I asked timidly where to go for a travel permit. She directed me toward a room at the end of the hall. Taking a deep breath, I knocked at the closed door.

A gruff voice sounded. *"Herein!"*

A big officer with piercing black eyes stared at me from behind a desk piled high with papers.

"Was wollen Sie?" he asked impatiently.

I explained in Dutch that my mother, two sisters, and I needed a permit to travel to Amsterdam, where we lived.

He raised thick eyebrows. "How did you get here?" he wanted to know.

I was afraid to tell him that we had traveled illegally on a barge, so I lied, "We walked."

"Then walk back," was the cold reply. The subject was closed, and he turned back to the papers on the desk.

I found myself back in the hall, shaken by the experience. So on a dark morning my mother, Cora, Anita, and I started out to return to Amsterdam, walking. We had some food from Oma and Opa and were bundled up with scarves, hats, and gloves, and extra paper in our shoes. My grandparents went out onto the street with us, tears in their eyes. They watched us and waved till we reached the corner. We were on our own again.

I remember very little of that road back. I do remember long days walking. Sometimes I carried Anita on my back because she was the weakest and had a hard time walking. At times we tried to hitchhike, even when we saw a German truck approaching. The people in front always shook their heads when they saw us standing on the side of the road holding up our hands. We spent the nights in barns along the way, and this only happened when the farmers were sympathetic. We begged for food, and even received something to eat every now and then.

There came a point when we were beyond feeling, beyond talking or planning. We just kept pushing along, putting one foot in front of the other, numb with misery. Life stopped, time ceased to exist. We just kept plodding along, from dark to dark.

After eight days we saw the first houses of Amsterdam. We arrived home to an icy cold house. Still dressed in our dirty clothes, we fell into bed and slept around the clock. This nightmare was over, but other nightmares were waiting to pounce upon us. At least my mother had seen her parents, and you might say we had an adventure.

Eight

THE HUNGER WINTER was in full force. The situation was getting worse and worse. The Allies were fighting in the southern part of Holland and had been stopped south of the Rhine. While some parts of the country had already been liberated, the western provinces were still occupied by the Germans. Rumors were circulating of people eating cats and dogs. Perhaps that was why we didn't see those animals any longer. There were actually people dying from hunger now. I have often wondered why our family survived.

In early December we heard about people who went to the farmers in the countryside to trade goods for food. Some farmers still had food at that time, hiding it from the Germans, and they would trade it for jewelry, fine linens, furniture, or expensive knick-knacks. So the stories went.

My mother came up with another plan—I should get on my bike, go to the countryside around Amsterdam, and do some trading for food. We still owned some good woolen blankets, a beautiful Belgian lace tablecloth, and even a couple of new dishtowels. For two days there had not been any food at all, then we received half a loaf of sticky black bread, reportedly made out of spinach seed. The situation was indeed dire, and I readily agreed to try to find food outside of Amsterdam. This time Cora, now fourteen, wanted to go with me.

Early one morning, as soon as it got light enough to see, we climbed on our old bikes with much-patched tires. Our good blankets were tied up on the luggage carriers for trading. We needed them ourselves, yet food was more important. It was bitter cold, but we were reasonably bundled up. Each of us had a soggy piece of black bread in our pockets for lunch. I had told our mother not to worry if we didn't get back before curfew, because we might have to stay in a barn somewhere if it got too late.

I had decided to go south, because of the many small towns and farm areas. We didn't talk much. We needed all our energy to keep pedaling. Cora was a quiet child and never had much to say. She suffered silently under the burdens of our difficult lives and never complained. The roads were mostly empty of traffic. The only vehicles we encountered were military cars and trucks. The ride gave me plenty of time to think.

I was nineteen now, and life seemed to have slipped away. Cold and hunger had become a way of life. I even learned that when you are always hungry the stomach eventually settles down to its empty existence and ceases to growl. Getting up in the morning meant another day without hope. Emotions like joy, laughter, contentment, or love had evaporated into a bleak cloud seeded with fear and intense loneliness.

In spite of all that, I still had dreams of happy people, warmth, and love. I yearned to love and be loved in return by someone strong, steady, and handsome. But then there was the reality, this life that was no longer a life. I was still very young but the burdens had doused any light I once saw. The concept of God had faded away. I sometimes thought, *If there is a God, how can He let all this happen?* Early childhood visions of the kind old gentleman hovering over me and taking care of me seemed unreal now. I forgot about the time I had missed the train that was attacked by a plane, or that we survived the trip on the barge, and even that my family and I were still alive.

We lived in cold darkness, with empty stomachs. Many years later I came to see the truth, the deepest darkness was the life without Jesus. Without sincere belief in the Savior there could not exist any light in a person's life. There would always be a vacuum no matter how good, comfortable, and pleasant life could be. It would, however, be many years before I came to this realization.

By mid-afternoon we had pedaled quite a distance without any luck at all. At the farms where we stopped either our knocking went unanswered or the door was slammed shut in our faces. Discouraged, Cora started crying, wishing we had stayed home. We could not make it back to the city before curfew, which was strictly enforced. What to do? No food, not able to go home, no roof for the night.

I remembered something. The family Rosmolen, whom we used to know years ago, lived in the small village of Woubrugge, not too far away. We had even spent a weekend with them once, and I had spent a vacation twice. Would they still remember us? Would we be able to find that place and possibly spend the night? We had to give it a try.

We plowed on with our rickety bikes, Cora's tears drying in this feeble glimmer of hope. We did come to the village, and after asking a few times we were directed toward the white house alongside the canal. I now remembered the narrow path leading toward the house, the smelly dairy farm across the road, and the little white fence with the gate. Everything looked the same. Too tired to hesitate, I knocked on the door. It was opened at once and I looked down at a small, plump woman with gray hair wearing a large striped apron. She stared intently at me for a few seconds and then her face lit up. She remembered me! I started to explain our situation but hardly had a chance to finish. We were invited to step inside. She briskly ordered someone inside the house to take care of our bikes and ushered us into a warm kitchen, which seemed to be full of people. Before we knew it we were sitting on chairs next to a big iron stove, upon which an enormous pot gave off a delicious smell.

"Just sit there, and warm up," she said with a smile. "We'll eat as soon as Hank comes home."

Hank was the boy I remembered. Last time I saw him those many years ago, he was a short kid about my age, and always rowing on the canal with his little canoe.

The large oval table was set for supper. Two more plates and two more chairs were added. Besides our friendly hostess there was the father of the house, sitting in a corner smoking a curved pipe, two younger men, one whom I recognized as the older brother, Bas, and a young woman holding a baby. That must be one of the sisters.

We were ravenous, and the smell of the rich food almost made me sick because my stomach had been empty so long.

The outside door opened, and a tall young man entered. Broad shoulders, dark wavy hair, and very handsome. He didn't seem a bit surprised to find two strangers sitting near the stove. The family gathered around the table. The pot was set in the middle next to a wooden board piled high with thick slices of brown bread. There was even a pot with butter.

The father started praying, which I remembered from earlier years. I glanced at Hank next to me. His eyes were closed, his head bowed. I quickly closed mine. The meal began. Being unaccustomed to rich, hot food, Cora and I couldn't eat very much, but we each ate two slices of the heavy bread, which tasted like the finest delicacy. After the meal the father read a long chapter from a worn Bible. I remembered this ritual from the past. Being full and warm, and oh, so tired, I had trouble staying awake. But some words caught my attention: "Blessed are they that hunger, because they shall be filled." I sat up straighter. I didn't know about blessings, but I was filled, all right, with stew and bread.

That evening a very strange thing happened. I recognized Hank as the vague person of my dreams, the one I yearned for, the one who would love me and care for me. We were sitting next to each other, and I felt a mystifying pull, a vibration between us. Later I learned he felt it too. It was like a live current passing between us. We didn't know it then, but it was love at first sight.

Cora and I spent the night upstairs under the slanted roof, on a softly crackling, sweet-smelling straw mattress under clean, warm blankets. The next morning we were treated to a wonderful breakfast. The same brown bread, now with homemade rhubarb jam and a real boiled egg for everyone. We even had hot fake tea, which was not bad at all.

It was time to return to Amsterdam. The family refused to accept our blankets. Instead, Hank loaded our bikes with apples, potatoes, a chunk of cheese, and homemade bread.

On the way back I was deeply shaken. I liked him! I loved him! I thought about him all the way home. And from then on, my first thought in the morning, and the last one at night, was of him.

There was a quivering in my soul, a smile on my lips. I saw beauty again in the shimmering frozen canals, the lacy bark of bare trees, the beautiful old houses leaning tiredly against each other. I felt a sense of hope, that perhaps there was still a future for me! I saw his face constantly before me. I was in love!

For the first time in many months, even years, I forgot about my stomach, the holes in my shoes, and even the enemy surrounding us. Life had returned to my soul, never to leave again. Troubles were still there, but the promise was alive.

Sometime in January we were totally out of food again. The gifts from Hank's family had long since been consumed, and even black market tulips were scarce. We had to think of something. My mother's friend, the captain's wife, whom we seldom saw, was not as bad off as we were because she had more money to spend on illegal foods. My mother asked her if she would be willing to take Cora and Anita into her home for a week while she and I foraged for food somewhere. She consented.

My mother and I rented a small handcart and went in search of food. As we walked, we decided to head to the north of Amsterdam, and so we went, taking turns pushing the little cart. This terrible winter, this Hunger Winter, was also one of the coldest on record.

It was a useless trip. It became a real nightmare without results. During the entire week we encountered only one place where we were kindly received, fed, and given a bed to sleep in. We discovered the people were Christians. They prayed for us, and with us, and read their Bible just like the Rosmolen family. It started me thinking. Was it different to be a Christian? Did they care more about others? Where did their kindness and love come from? Was it because they read the Bible? What would it take to become like them? Hank was a Christian, or at least it appeared so the time I was in his home. I felt so empty, like a great void existed inside of me. I hungered, not only for something to eat, but for something more. What was it? I felt there was more to life than this empty struggle. I used to believe there was a God and that he was with me, hovering over me. What had happened to those feelings? Of course, that was many years ago. I was grown now and this war made everything different. *Who could have loving thoughts in times like these?* I kept thinking as we plodded from farmhouse to farmhouse.

After several days we returned home disappointed and disillusioned. We barely spoke. It was too much to talk about all this useless trying to get food. Back in the city, we dropped off the empty little handcart and went home.

My mother opened the door with her key. Things looked different. Puzzled, we looked around and thought at first that we were in the wrong house. The rug in the hall was gone, as well as the few old coats that had been hanging on knobs. We walked into the sitting room at the front of the apartment. It was stripped bare. The only thing left was the upright piano, which obviously had been moved away from the wall. My mother screamed and ran into the bedroom. Two beds with nothing but the bare springs were all we saw. Gone were the blankets, the pillows, the sheets, and the mattresses. She screamed again and flew to the kitchen. The dishes were gone, all the pots and pans, the small table, the oil burner. Even the small pieces of wood piled on the floor to burn in our makeshift stove were gone. The closets with our remaining clothes were empty. Even Anita's toys were gone. We were left with an empty house and the clothes on our back. Everything had been stolen, except that which could not be easily carried.

We were numb, too shocked to speak. The screaming had stopped. We stood there, hanging on to each other. My mother sat down on the floor and sobbed, a heartrending sound. And I just kept standing there. What would we do next?

The days after our return are hidden in a fog. Things happened but did not register. I went to the police, but they just shrugged.

"We can't go after that," I was told. "It happens too often."

Nine

WE HAD REACHED the ultimate bottom and there was only one way to go—up. People in the office where I still worked gathered up enough clothes for our family to dress us all; nice things too, because most of them came from wealthy families. From the organization that took care of seamen's families we received bedding and some furniture. In just a few days we had the basic necessities to live, all donated.

My mother wanted to move again, because it had become scary to live in this apartment, where thieves had broken in. I never understood how she always found places for us to live, but she did. This time we found a second-floor apartment far from Amsterdam's center, away from the Jewish neighborhood, and in a rather pretty area. There were trees in this street. I had to walk much farther to the office, but that was a minor thing. We picked up our lives again, and those lives were full of fear more than ever. There were places in many neighborhoods now where people could receive food. Twice a week we could go there with a container and receive some soupy stuff, mostly cabbage and even some potatoes thrown in. Sometimes the potatoes had been frozen and tasted sweet, rather a rotten taste. With the very meager rations and what I could buy on the black market once in a while, we did survive.

The Dutch resistance groups were very active these last months of the war, blowing up bridges and trains, and assassinating German officials. Hostages were taken by the Germans, and whenever sabotage occurred they were taken to public squares and shot execution style by firing squads, while the Dutch were forced to watch.

On one of those times, Cora, still only fourteen years old, was forced to watch the shooting of a large group of hostages. After that great trauma, she became even more quiet and still.

The winter slowly gave way to a hesitant spring. Green buds started to appear on trees, and green sprouts peeped out of the ground in the parks. The sun turned a little warmer, and the blue, clear skies brightened moods a little.

On a fresh, cool, and crisp Saturday afternoon, feeling a bit cheerful because of the signs of spring, I came home from the office where I had worked till noon.

My mother was sweeping the sidewalk in front of the door. She straightened up and gave me a strange look.

"You have company," she told me.

"Company? Who?" I wanted to know.

"Go and find out."

Who would visit me? I didn't have any friends. It flashed through my mind, could it be Hank? I had written him a note after the robbery. Mail was still being delivered, even though it was slow. He had not responded, however. I thought about him day and night, realizing that I might never see him again and feeling a deep sadness because of it.

I climbed the stairs and opened the door to our apartment. When I entered the living room, I stood thunderstruck. Hank rose up from a chair. There he stood, broad and handsome, with a big grin. We just looked at each other. Neither of us knew what to say. For many seconds that seemed like hours, we didn't move.

"I came to see you. I brought food," he said.

I couldn't talk. My heart was trying to jump out of my chest. We kept staring. Finally, he spoke again.

"Would you like an apple or a sandwich?"

"A s-s-sandwich?" I stuttered.

Then I noticed Cora and Anita who were watching us with great interest. They were both eating. He handed me a neatly wrapped sandwich—the well-remembered brown bread with thick slices of cheese. I ate it right then and there, still standing.

And so began our courtship. He came to Amsterdam a few times after that, always unexpected, and always bringing food. He did a very dangerous thing by coming to see me. The Germans were forever picking up boys and men and moving them to Germany. Hank was a member of the resistance, and was still listed as not having reported to go to Germany when he was drafted.

Hank's family had expressed very strong opinions that he must be insane to go to Amsterdam, just to see some girl, risking his life. Hank was a very determined fellow, and besides, he was in love too.

That first time he stayed till Monday morning, sleeping on the hard floor. We went for walks most of the time just to be together, away from everyone else. We talked and talked. On a street corner with people passing by, he suddenly grabbed me, and we kissed long and hard for the first time. We could not hold off any longer.

When he left he promised to come back. I could hardly believe what had happened. I had known that I was in love, but now somebody loved me back. He had told me so. Was this all for real? Was I dreaming?

How changed my life was! I was happy—for the first time I was happy! It was like floating on a cloud! Nothing bothered me any longer. The war would be over soon, and now there could be a bright future for me—with Hank. I didn't know how or when it would really happen, but I didn't bother with details. It would happen, of that I was sure.

The end of the war came nearer and the Germans, knowing that their cause was lost, became more brutal. They hunted and caught Jews, freedom fighters, and resistance leaders, and shot many of them regardless of gender or age. Hank became more and more concerned about the safety of my family and me, and went to have a talk with his oldest sister, Cor, and brother-in-law, Hannes, who lived in an isolated area on a farm south of Amsterdam. It was decided that my mother, Cora, and Anita would live with them for the duration of the war, and I would move into Hank's home in Woubrugge, because there was not enough room for all four of us. Hannes worked for several farmers, and they still had food, if not plentiful. Hank and his brother Bas would also help with supplies.

Our bare-bones apartment was locked, I took a leave of absence from the office, and with our few belongings we left on our bicycles. My mother and sisters went to Hank's sister's home in Badhoevendorp, and I went with Hank to Woubrugge.

A new life began for me. I ate three times a day, slept with Pat, his youngest sister, upstairs under the roof, helped with chores, and spent the rest of the time with Hank. We got to know each other in an everyday setting, and were more in love every day. We took walks along the dike. He took me sailing in his little sailboat, which had replaced the canoe.

He informed me that he liked girls who liked sailing.

"That's me!" I answered bravely, cringing at the look of the waves on the canal.

The first time he took me sailing, I really came to know who he was—a man. It was quite breezy that afternoon on the lake but also very beautiful. The choppy water reflected the bright blue of the sky, and the waves were crested with white foam. Fluffy clouds were marching in from the west, announcing more wind to come.

In the bottom of the sleek little boat topped by billowing sails I sat on a pillow and was totally fascinated by Hank. I could not keep my eyes away from him. He sat there at the helm, ropes wound around his hands. Those hands—so broad, large, and strong! His green eyes were stern and alert, the eyes of an eagle, I thought. He scanned the water, the skies, and the sails. Nothing escaped him. Nothing ever did. He was totally absorbed in keeping the boat level. His powerful legs in the khaki shorts were braced against the side. His black hair was blowing in the wind, and his tanned skin had the healthy glow of someone who spent lots of time outdoors. Only twenty-one he was, but already a man in the finest sense of the word. It was hard to imagine him ever having been a boy.

He smiled at me, relaxing a bit, and his eyes were full of tenderness. I felt loved and cherished, amazed that such a man had chosen me!

His job in life, he told me once years later, was to take care of me, and that is why he was born. Next to God, I became the most important person in his life.

One of the many memory pictures engraved in my heart is of that day, of the young man with the eyes of an eagle, and the strong hands, conquering the waves and the wind at the helm of a little sailboat.

When we were not sailing, we loved to go for walks along the canal. We would go quite a distance, and sit on the dike in the grass. One afternoon, as we just had settled down on our favorite spot, a large barge was slowly drifting by in the canal. Suddenly, a plane descended from the clouds, and we heard the sound of gunfire. The barge was being attacked. The bullets came down in streams and were hitting the dike. We jumped up and ran down to the field below, the bullets following us left and right, making little puffs of dirt in the grass. They plopped in front of us, behind us, all around us. The barge, the main target, was hit all along the deck. We didn't wait to see the damage but ran home. Arriving at the house, out of breath and hardly able to talk, we stared at each other.

"Do you realize," Hank asked, "that we could have been killed just now?"

I couldn't answer. My teeth were chattering, and I was too shaken.

That was yet another time that I was spared during my life.

That spring Hank tried to teach me how to sail, and I was doing rather well. How different life had become! I was out of Amsterdam, away from the depressing circumstances. I had food to eat, and I lived under the same roof as the one I loved. I never thought about what would happen in the future, only about the day at hand.

Hank loved to go sailing when there was a strong wind. I called it a storm. I was scared but cheerfully went along because, as he had told me, he loved girls who loved sailing. When it was blowing really hard we had to hang over the side holding onto the ropes, trying to bring balance to the boat so we wouldn't capsize. I couldn't even swim, having always been afraid of water, but wouldn't confess how afraid I was.

One time, out on the lake which was calm for once, he told me, "I could never love a girl who didn't love God."

I had learned that God was very real to him. I had discarded the concept of God due to the terrible suffering I had witnessed. How could I start loving God now? I remembered the small child who had believed in God as a kind old gentleman hovering over her. When exactly had I lost this feeling? I knew that several times during the last years my life had been spared. Had God done that? Was he still hovering over me?

Hank knew about my family, and he was aware that I didn't know anything about being a Christian. He never let a chance go by to tell me about Jesus. He was a great preacher during those times. We would moor the boat in a little spot in the tall reeds, and he would explain God to me, and Jesus Christ, heaven, and faith. I wanted to believe, mostly because he believed. I loved it when he talked about God and Jesus. I admired everything he stood for.

I also wondered if we would ever be married after the war was over. He never talked about it. We were so-called "going together," and "going steady." But where would it lead?

One bright afternoon out on the lake, sailing along, he said to me, "A good marriage is not bad."

"No," I agreed.

"That's settled then." He nodded a couple of times, with a big smile, and started looking at the sails again.

I wondered if this was a proposal. I thought it was. I hoped it was. Could I consider us engaged then? A little flustered, I looked out over the water. I had dared to dream, and it seemed the dream would become reality. But it was a strange proposal indeed. Being a true romantic, I had often dreamt of being in love and being proposed to in a very special way. It would be evening; a full moon would be shining with stars sparkling all over a deep blue sky. The young man in question would take my hand, look deeply into my eyes, and softly speak of love and marriage.

I had never imagined that I would have a sailboat as a competitor during a marriage proposal. In the days that followed, however, I became joyfully aware that Hank was convinced that we would marry, that it was all settled, and that it would be forever.

I spent the remaining time of the war at Hank's home, while my mother and sisters were taken care of by Cor and Hannes. The situation in the cities was desperate. Children from the big cities like Rotterdam and Amsterdam were transported to the northern provinces where there was more food for them. The Swedish Red Cross got involved and negotiated with the Germans to let Swedish ships loaded with grain, butter, and white bread come to the cities. To divide this among the starving population was quite an assignment, and it was done with great precision.

In the month of April the American Lancasters and Flying Fortresses were allowed to fly over western Holland to drop cases and burlap bags with food for the population.

I will never forget the immense thrill of those great planes flying low over the countryside, without being shot at. People yelled and waved and jumped up and down, tears streaming down their faces. Hank and Bas climbed on the roof of the house with a large Dutch flag, red, white, and blue. They held it up and waved it at the passing planes. The planes came lower yet, and the boys declared that they saw the pilots waving back.

Outside the towns and villages on grassy fields the first crates of food were dropped. In Woubrugge the mayor and constable arrived right away, accompanied by many villagers. It became a riot. People were trying to get at the food first, and there was even fighting going on. There were the greedy ones, the selfish ones, the fighters, the bullies, and the timid ones who held back. It became quite ugly. I had learned these last years that hunger brings out either the best in people, or the worst. With much shouting and pushing, and help from the village authorities, every family got its share.

I remember that first American food—large cans of powdered milk, tins of Spam, powdered eggs, and large cans that read "shortening." We had absolutely no idea what that was. It didn't taste like butter. It was white. We wondered what Americans used it for. Hank's mother discovered you could fry with it, but it didn't taste very good on bread. The biggest surprise of all was chocolate—real chocolate in large slabs.

For years, chocolate had been a forgotten item. Hank's father divided the chunk of chocolate among the members of the household, except I did not get any because his father declared that I did not belong. Hank promptly broke his piece in two and gave me half of it. My vague suspicion that Hank Senior did not like me became truth at that time.

It was May again, May 5, 1945, and the day had arrived when the German garrison that was housed in Woubrugge left. Germany had lost its war, and the soldiers had orders to leave. The population lined the bridge across the canal and watched them go. They were a sorry lot. Tired, disillusioned, shabby, and hungry. They walked, heads bowed, dragging their feet. Most people watched silently although some jeered and shouted insults. We watched them go till they disappeared out of sight.

Five long years had passed. The Netherlands as we had known it, no longer existed. Cities were bombed, the harbors destroyed, most of the Jews and many others were gassed in concentration camps. The economy was in chaos. The Germans had bombed the dikes in the southern part of the country that held back the sea, so salt water had flooded the fertile lands. There were few jobs and much poverty.

The Dutch are a tough and stubborn lot. They would never be the same, but they could build again. A new world waited, a different world but not a better one. We could never recapture the life that existed before the war. The war years stood like a giant mountain dividing the life of the country into before and after. What kind of life would evolve in the new time of peace? What would lie ahead for Hank and me?

PART II

Ten

NOTHING GOOD WILL come out of war, any war. There is the aftermath, and the consequences of suffering and persecution. Life will not automatically turn back to the way it was. People have changed, some for the better, some for the worst. They have known hunger, fear, loss of loved ones. Their senses have been dulled. Cynicism often takes the place of compassion and love for others. A hardness comes over a people that have suffered much, and it now becomes commonplace to think first about me, me, and me.

It was spring again, and there rose up a collective sigh of relief. No more bombs, no knocks on the door in the middle of the night. Freedom.

First, there existed a matter to be dealt with. During the war quite a few Dutch girls and women had fraternized with the enemy. They had been walking about arm in arm with German soldiers. They were seen in movie houses and in parks. Their names had been noted and remembered. After the Germans left these women were hunted down by the Dutch. That turned into an ugly thing. I witnessed them being tied to trees, with much jeering and screaming from the excited onlookers. Then their hair was cut off completely, to the bare scalp. Their crying, pleading, and sobbing didn't help. If you had dated a German, you lost your hair.

Some of these women would grab a handful of their hair after the scalping and push it under a scarf, showing a bit of it. I didn't believe that anyone, no matter what they had done, deserved such an extremely humiliating punishment.

I saw it happen once and felt sick afterwards, also guilty, as if I myself had done this to them.

The western part of Holland, after finally being liberated, was mostly occupied by Canadian troops. They behaved worse than the Germans had where women were concerned. In the cities no woman was safe on the street after dark, and before long people were wishing to be liberated from the Canadians. German soldiers had not been permitted to force their attentions on the female population. They only approached a woman who wanted to be noticed, when the signs were clear and open.

Curfew became a thing of the past. The old street organs were hauled out onto the streets again, and in the evening loud music could be heard accompanied by wild dancing, till all hours of the night. Abandoned behavior became the mode of entertainment.

A shocking discovery was the plight of the Jews and others in the German concentration camps. The Russian and Allied armies, discovering the camps in Poland and Eastern Germany, had filmed what they found there, and soon the films were shown all over Europe. People sat in movie theaters and stared dumbfounded at the screens. Wobbling skeletons barely resembling humans, bulldozers moving mountainous piles of skulls and bones! We looked at pictures of gas chambers where the Jews had been reduced to ashes, which were then dumped into rivers.

We had heard rumors, but no one had known the truth, and now we saw it. I am convinced that what happened to the people in the concentration camps was the most devastating of the entire war. We were bombed, starving, had lived with great fear, and many were shot or imprisoned, but the sight of the remains of those people who had lived among us and who were part of us was beyond comprehension. Many of the Dutch had hidden Jews during the war, fought for them, and protected them. Now we learned what had happened to them. Miraculously, a few survived and returned to pick life up again.

One of the people who returned was the father of Anne Frank. She had kept a diary, and when the Germans raided the secret hiding place of the Frank family, they left the diary behind. It was found and kept by a friend, and after the war it was published as a book, and became the classic *The Diary of Anne Frank*. It swept the world.

When the address of the hiding place became known, I remembered walking past the place while going to work at the brewery office. I wondered, did she see me walking by in freedom, on my way to work, while she perhaps was looking through the attic window?

My mother and sisters went back to live in the apartment in Amsterdam, and my mother wanted me to come too. I felt obligated to go back to my job to earn some money for the family.

Hank and I had to separate. I moved back to Amsterdam and Hank stayed behind in Woubrugge. It was easy to get my old job back and we tried to pick up life where we had left it.

I was lost without Hank, and it became a habit that on Saturday afternoon I would bicycle from Amsterdam to Woubrugge, about 40 kilometers, to spend the weekend. I would return on Sunday evening. Sometimes Hank would come to the city. He was trying hard to find work, which in this destroyed economy was not easy. We were still "going steady," but there was no talk about marriage.

During that summer a letter from America arrived. It had been delivered to the address of my grandparents, and they had sent it on. The boy I had written to before the war was anxious to hear from me, to know if I had survived, and what I was doing. He mentioned somewhere in the letter, why don't you come to America? Six little words which changed the future.

Yes, why don't I, I thought. The next time I saw Hank I said, "Would you like to go to America?"

He looked rather strangely at me. "Whatever gave you that idea?"

I explained, and mentioned that there was not much to live for in our destroyed country, and that it would be just great to go to America, a land where I had always wanted to go. I used to love the American movies before the war, especially the cowboy movies, and as a young girl I collected movie star pictures by the hundreds. Hank, rather dubious, admitted that it would be something different, perhaps with a better future.

At the first opportunity I headed for the American Consulate in Rotterdam. I told the friendly man behind a big desk that my fiancé and I wanted to go to America. He smiled, and shook his head.

"That is not so easy, young lady. You and about a million other Europeans want to go to America. You will have to wait till your quota number comes up."

I didn't quite understand what he meant, but I said, "That is fine. We will wait."

He handed me some papers to fill out.

The next time I saw Hank, I informed him that it would take a long time to be able to go to America, and just to forget about it.

In October, 1945 my stepfather, Gerard Appel, came back from the sea. I had hoped I would never see him again, but there he was. He had been on an oil tanker during the war years, and had survived two torpedo attacks. He moved right in, of course, and with him came his disagreeable personality. He immediately decided, backed up by my mother, that I had to break up with Hank because Hank was a Christian, and therefore a coward and a nobody. Terrible arguments and fights started. My mother, who knew how much I loved Hank, was all in agreement with Gerard. She had spent the last months of the war in safety at Hank's sister's home, but now she was all against that family, especially Hank. They both demanded I break if off.

My mother wanted to move once again, and we ended up in a larger apartment near the Rijksmuseum. Gerard was home all the time, having received some kind of a pension because of his work during the war years. I decided it was worse having him home than during the war years, when at least he was gone.

Whenever Hank came to see me he was treated like dirt or ignored. Hank's family was not exactly fond of me either. I overheard his father tell his brother-in-law once that I was the worst mistake Hank ever made, and at the time his sisters were not happy with me either, although in later years we became good friends.

At about this time I received shattering news. My friend Fietje had died in Ravensbrueck, a German concentration camp for women, three days before the camp was liberated. It was the infamous camp where experiments on women were conducted. Her sister Marianne had survived and was taken by the Swedish Red Cross people to Sweden where she was nursed back to physical health. She brought home the message of Fietje's death. She also told how Fietje had encouraged and helped and cared for women till her death. She was loved by all.

My small struggles during the war years seemed like nothing compared to what had happened to Fietje. She was the only one of her family who did not survive.

In the spring of 1946, Hank and I decided to get married. My situation at home was intolerable, and my parents continued to harass me about dropping Hank. Hank had found a job in a laundry, which was not much, but with my wages from the brewery office we would manage. Housing was very tight, too, because the Netherlands was far from being on its feet again. Food was still rationed, so were textiles, and shoes, even household goods like pots and pans. A marriage license would allow us to buy the main necessities.

We found an apartment. The living and dining room combination was on the second floor, and our bedroom was three flights up. We had to share the bathroom and kitchen with two other couples. In spite of all that we were lucky to have found something. When we informed the family that we were going to get married the following month, on April 3rd, a howl went up on both sides. We invited them all to come to the wedding if they wanted to. I was only twenty, and according to Dutch law I had to have permission from a parent or guardian. Hank had just turned twenty-two.

When the day of the wedding dawned it turned out to be a beautiful spring day. There was not a chance for a church wedding since neither family went to church, for different reasons, so we were married at the courthouse in Amsterdam. My grandparents had arrived the day before to be at my wedding, but my mother did not allow them to come to the courthouse with us. My sisters also were told to stay home. Hank's parents came, with his sisters Cor and Pat, and Pat's husband, Tony, and his brother Bas and wife Jo.

The ceremony was short, cold, and businesslike, just the signing of papers. But we were deliriously happy in spite of the surroundings. We were married, and that was all that mattered! My mother did invite us to come home with her, because my grandmother had insisted on having a little luncheon for us.

A funny thing happened on the way to her home. We went by streetcar, which was the main means of transportation. At a certain stop Hank said suddenly, "This is where we get off."

He pushed me out of the streetcar, and was at the point of following me, when he realized that it was a couple of blocks too early. He remained on the streetcar with the rest of the family, and there they went, leaving me behind standing on the sidewalk. Hank had the dumbest look on his face. He weakly waved at me, and I am sure I had a scowl on my face. I had to walk several city blocks, until I came to the street where my mother lived. There stood Hank, surrounded by his family, all looking a little sheepish. The bride had finally shown up!

We were all hungry and ready for something to eat. When we entered the apartment, my mother and stepfather were waiting. They put on their coats and hats, and said, "We are not going to congratulate you, because it is not worth it to us."

Without acknowledging any of Hank's family, even his parents, they promptly left, slamming the door behind them.

That evening we were truly alone for the first time in a place of our own. Hank had always saved whatever money he earned, and we had been able to buy some furnishings—a large straw mat for the linoleum-covered floor, a square table with four chairs, two small easy chairs, and a tiny chest. Our bedroom way upstairs had a double bed, two chairs, and a small table at the wall. We also had a clothes closet, and as in all Dutch bedrooms, a large washbowl with running water.

That night we didn't need to be separated any longer, and when I woke up in the morning, snuggled against Hank, I realized that I had never known that such happiness existed.

Our life together began. Hank had his job at the laundry and I at the office. We went to work on our bicycles, since both of us worked downtown. As was customary in Holland, we worked Saturdays till noon. As soon as we came home we packed some clothes and headed for Woubrugge. I was not always so happy about going there, because his father barely spoke to me even after our wedding. I never felt much at home with Hank's family, but his little sailboat was there, and he didn't like life in the big city at all. His heart was in the village and on the water, especially on the lake. He wanted to go sailing every weekend, weather permitting or not permitting, whatever the case might be.

Hank taught me serious sailing that summer, and surprisingly I became quite good at it. Never, though, did I feel comfortable. I could hardly swim and was still scared of the water.

When I was a child, and into my teenage years I often had the same dream: I was running and someone was following me. I ran and ran, until I fell into water—a deep and dark and very cold body of water. I went down and down, deeper and deeper, and drowned. I would wake up trembling and shaking out of this nightmare, still feeling surrounded by some terrible danger. When I met Hank the dreams stopped. I finally felt secure and that was the end of the nightmares.

For the rest of my life I have always had a fear of water, and no matter how I tried to learn to swim to please Hank, I became petrified if the water got so deep that I could no longer feel any bottom. In spite of that, Hank loved sailing and he loved girls who liked sailing, so I sailed.

Eleven

THE FOLLOWING YEAR was a time of discovery. We had spent the last months of the war together at his home, walking and talking, seeing the end of the war become reality. Then we visited each other on weekends, lived with ridicule and disapproval from family members, and now we were together for good. And we discovered each other.

Hank learned that I was extremely insecure, always afraid that his love for me would not last. I fussed and fretted about that, sometimes making him angry, sometimes hurting his feelings. He understood, however. I had never been used to being loved, so he made it his priority to convince me that yes, he loved me, and of course, it would be forever.

I found out that I had married a very bossy person who liked to get his way. He was a born leader and fully expected me to accept that. I didn't really mind, because it made me feel taken care of in the best sense. He was also quite stubborn, which was the very thing that made him come after me in Amsterdam that first time, against his parents' wishes.

We didn't like the same foods. Hank had a sweet tooth, I could easily forget about sweet things. He hated mustard, I loved it. He loathed fish, I could eat it seven days a week. We were so happy, however, that all these little differences didn't amount to anything serious. There existed that powerful attraction between us so that we did not feel complete without each other. We rushed home after work, impatient to be together again.

Sometimes we talked about the future with vague feelings of uncertainty. Both of us hoped to get ahead in life, but there didn't seem to exist much of a chance for that in the aftermath of the war.

The economy was still very much down. Housing was almost nonexistent for married couples getting started. Certain foods, textiles, and shoes were still rationed. Many items, such as cheese and butter, were for export and not for the Dutch people. The government wanted to pay off its debt to the United States first, before relaxing trade. After the war the Marshall Plan had been established to aid the European countries, and the Netherlands would be the first country to pay off its debt to the United States.

Our living arrangement in the apartment with the two other couples proved far from ideal. Meat was still rationed and we were able to buy it only once a week. One Sunday I was cooking two pork chops in the community kitchen. While I was setting the table in our room, the meat was stolen right out of my frying pan. The bathroom was forever occupied, and one of the other women had the habit of taking a bath with the door unlocked. When the other husband walked in on her, there she sat, naked and giggling, and a nasty fight erupted between the two couples. Hank and I thought it was time to look for another place.

Unexpectedly, his brother-in-law, who was married to Hank's sister Marie, and who worked in a bank, found Hank a job as a teller. We would have to move to Haarlem. That was fine with us, because Hank never liked Amsterdam too well.

Haarlem was an old city full of history and ancient buildings, and we were happy to settle down there. The apartment was not much better but at least we had more privacy. The tiny living area barely held a table and two chairs. There was a kitchen, a water closet, and we slept next to the coal bins where the coal was stored for all the people in the building. We lived right around the corner from the watch shop where Corrie Ten Boom had lived.

Hank worked in the bank, and I found another office job. After the turmoil of the war years, life settled down into a routine, with not much hope of a change for the better.

One day a letter arrived. It was an official document from the American Consulate in Rotterdam, forwarded from Woubrugge. Our quota number was up, and we could get started on our papers to go to America on an immigrant visa. The letter contained a long list of requirements:

We needed an affidavit of support from an American citizen, so that we would not become a liability to the American government.

We needed papers of good conduct from every police department in every town we had lived in from the age of fifteen.

We needed medical proof that we did not have tuberculosis or a venereal disease. And last, we had to swear that we never were communists, or Nazis, or were homosexual.

Such were the requirements for prospective immigrants in 1948.

Hank and I were thunderstruck! We had not thought about America since that time I had gone to the Consulate in Rotterdam and filled out some papers. That was about three years previous. I had written to the Moorman family occasionally and received letters back, but there had not been any mention about going there.

We took an inventory of our life in Holland. We could not hope for adequate housing for several years. For Hank there existed not much future. He had an eighth-grade education and could not expect to find a good job. The war had totally interrupted his schooling, as it had for so many young Dutch men. We were both ambitious with dreams of climbing up in life. I also wanted to get away from my family and all the harassment about our marriage, which never seemed to stop.

Hank and I never had to think very long about great decisions. In important things we were of one mind. So, just like that, we decided to start making plans to go to America. First of all, I would write to Fred and Hazel Moorman to ask for the affidavit of support. We both knew we could not expect that these people would consent to do this. How could they possibly vouch for two people they had never met, didn't even know, and then be responsible for them probably for years to come?

I wrote the letter in my very elementary English, explaining what we needed. I informed them that we would fully understand if they felt they could not grant our request. After all, we could be a couple of "gangsters" (a word I had learned from American movies), and that we could get them in all kinds of trouble. It must have been a hilarious letter. The Moorman family had a good laugh over it and kept it for many years.

We decided to wait for an answer before we would tell our families. Amazingly, the answer came very quickly—a thick, very large envelope with all the necessary documents, signed and notarized. Fred Moorman, the head of the family, was a plumber who earned three thousand dollars a year, and that was sufficient to guarantee our support.

Now the time came to tell our parents of the great plans we had. As expected, we created an uproar! My parents scoffed, laughed, and said, "You will never get there, and even if you would, you will be back without him within a year!"

"Him," meaning my husband.

Hank's parents and other family members thought that it was the craziest thing they ever heard. Nobody ever went to America just like that, and it just would be impossible. Hank's father declared that it was all my fault.

Four months later, on December 27, 1948, we boarded the SS *Noordam* of the Holland America Line at her berth in Rotterdam. It had been a very busy time of acquiring all the necessary papers, selling furniture, buying our one-way tickets to New York City, and setting aside enough money for the train ride to Kansas. We kept up a lively correspondence with our sponsors in America, so they were informed of everything. It seemed they were just as excited as we were. They had written that we could live with them until we found jobs and a place of our own.

I have often thought in later years what a courageous thing it was to leave our country to go to a totally strange place far away across the ocean, leaving everything familiar behind, even our families. Hank did not know one word of English; we did not have jobs, and hardly had any money to start with.

Hank felt that the Lord directed all this. I agreed. After living with Hank for over two years I had arrived at a great awareness that God indeed existed, that He directed our lives, and that Jesus Christ was His Son who died for our sins. I was convinced that the Lord had watched over me all during the war years, always by my side in the direst situations, and above all, had given Hank to me. Who would ever have predicted in our childhood years when we played together on that heap of gravel that one day we would become husband and wife? God already had decided then that we would be together for the rest of our lives. And now, leaving Holland to go to a totally new country must all have been part of God's great master plan for us.

The day we left for America was a raw, gray day. The ship lay there proudly topped by her two yellow smokestacks, with the colors green-white-green encircling the top. It seemed enormous to us, although it was one of the smaller ships of the Holland America Line, part passenger liner and part freighter.

Almost Hank's entire family, my stepfather and sisters, and even my grandparents saw us off. My mother had chosen to stay at home.

When we walked onto the gangplank up to the ship, I knew that was it, the thing had been done, and there was no turning back. We joined a crowd of people standing at the railing waving to the people in the terminal, who were watching from behind tall windows. We searched out our families and waved, too. They seemed so small, so separated from us already.

I shivered in my winter coat and glanced at Hank. His face was serious, tense, and quite pale. A few days earlier he had received his smallpox inoculation, and he did not feel very well. I had received mine when I was six, before entering grade school.

The powerful engines started to throb and the ship slowly moved away from the pier. People were shouting and frantically waving all around us. We saw our families getting smaller and smaller, until finally they were gone from our view. It was bitter cold, but we remained at the railing watching the countryside glide by, until we arrived at the last point of the land, Hoek van Holland. It was a strange sensation, watching that last little strip of our country fade away.

Here we were, it was just us now. We were young, full of courage and spirit, and excited to make a new life for ourselves.

As I looked out over the restless water, it was hard to believe that it had only been eight years since the war had broken out in our country. So much had happened in that span of time. We each experienced different things but had grown up and found each other. What a story to tell our children some day!

Hank let out a deep sigh and said, "Come on, let's find our cabin and warm up."

We were directed to our very nice cabin, where our suitcases were waiting for us at the foot of the twin beds. We sat down on the beds and stared at each other.

"Well, sweetheart, we did it!" Hank smiled at me.

"We sure did," I answered, surprised that I felt a little shaky and nervous about the whole adventure. Were we sure we knew what we were doing? Of course, it was a little late to start asking a question like that. We had made this important decision to emigrate, and that was it. No use to start wondering now if we had done the right thing.

Our voyage across the Atlantic became the experience of a lifetime. The worst storm in twenty-five years hit us, starting on the third day. After the last glimpse of land had disappeared from sight, we saw nothing but dark green and black constantly moving water, restless and (to me) threatening. We were sure that it would stay that way all the way to New York City. In spite of my fear of water, the strong engines at the heart of this large ship gave me a sense of security.

Our first lunch in the great dining room was quite a surprise. We were served food we had not seen for years: meats, oranges, and other fruit, cheeses, and desserts made with chocolate. No shortage of delicious food existed on board the *Noordam*. Hank, however, could not enjoy our first meals because he was getting sicker from the smallpox vaccination. He was a bit nauseated and feverish, and could not enjoy the food as much as he wanted to.

For the first few days we walked the deck wrapped in our winter coats, or sat in deck chairs huddled under plaid blankets. It was great fun watching our fellow passengers. We often encountered an American woman, very chic and slender, who walked the deck with three small dogs on a leash. We kept seeing another American, very tall with wild hair, who we imagined could easily pass for an artist. I didn't know why I thought of him as such, except he wore many bracelets, an extravagant multicolored scarf, and a flamboyant French beret over one eye.

On the third day the storm hit! And it proved to be the worst storm in the North Atlantic in twenty-five years! The roiling waves turned into giant mountains of dark water, cresting with furious foam. Never could we have imagined such waves! Some grew higher than the top of the ship, slamming over her with crashing, earsplitting sounds. It was the scariest thing ever, especially for someone like me, who was already afraid of water! The decks were off limits and we had to stay inside. Hank, still not feeling well, became terribly seasick. I, too, started vomiting because of the wild motion of the ship.

Hank took to his bed, but I did try the dining room a few times. We had paid for this wonderful food, and I was going to eat it, sick or not. The round tables had been edged with raised borders several inches high. They prevented the plates from sliding into our laps. It became quite interesting to try to eat soup from a bowl that kept sliding across the table.

After several days of this frightening storm, the waves finally died down. The voyage was supposed to have lasted eight days, but because of the storm it lasted eleven. One day the ship did not make any progress at all because it was too dangerous, we were told. When the storm died down people started feeling better, and even Hank perked up. The dining room, which had been half empty, started to fill up again and we saw people we had not met before.

When we came on deck the first calm morning, we saw another ship far out on the horizon. Our passengers started hollering and waving, even if it was too far away to notice us. Another survivor!

Twelve

DURING THE STORM and all the seasickness, the New Year had come and gone, barely noticed. The year 1949 had arrived, and on January 7 the *Noordam* sailed into New York Harbor. As we slowly passed the Statue of Liberty, I remember thinking, why did the most memorable days in my life always seem to start with gray and damp weather? Most of the passengers stood at the rail, huddled in coats and blankets, eyes fixed on the symbol of freedom. She rose so proudly out of the water, hand held high, lighting the way with her lamp. It amazed me she was green, a soft, almost bluish green. Later I learned she was covered with mildew from the dampness.

Hank and I linked arms, standing close together and sharing a peculiar sensation. All these many days at sea we had been drifting in a no-man's land between two continents, between two kinds of lives, between the past and the future. Now, right before us loomed the first sign that we had indeed arrived at the latter.

"Well, sweetheart," he said, squeezing my arm, "here we are."

I nodded, speechless, and felt a vague sense of fear in what we had done.

The harbor looked much like the one we had left behind in Rotterdam, except bigger, and at this side of the world towered the skyscrapers we had heard so much about.

Customs officials climbed on board. We were questioned, and our papers examined. Finally, we were allowed to go on shore and there we stood, on American ground.

We didn't know what to do, and just stared at all the hustle and bustle of the debarking passengers, being engulfed by a totally strange language. My proper, British-schoolgirl English had not prepared me for what I heard now. It didn't even sound like English. Hank, the strength of our marriage, didn't speak the language at all and would depend upon me to get us through whatever happened next.

A fellow Dutch passenger who had befriended us on the ship walked up to us and informed us that a bus would take us to Grand Central Station. He was going to his brother in Chicago, and also headed for the station. We picked up our luggage and followed him to a large bus, already loading people. I muttered to the driver something about Grand Central Station and he nodded, answering something. Our suitcases were loaded up and we sat side by side in the bus, numb with anxiety, bewildered by all the strangeness. The bus traveled through crowded streets with tall, narrow houses, and people and cars everywhere. After some time the driver stopped and pointed to us. He said something about "station."

There it stood, the next phase of our journey. I remember a giant building, with more bustling people. People sat behind counters, obviously selling tickets. I parked Hank with our luggage near one of the counters, and tried to buy two tickets for Lawrence, Kansas. The girl didn't understand me, and I had no idea what she was telling me. She remained friendly, and finally, after much trying, her smile widened as recognition dawned and she said, "Oh, you mean Kaaansas!" It was the first time I discovered that the American *a* sounded quite different from the British *a*.

The train trip through wintery landscape to Kansas remains a blurred memory. We had bought a sack full of sausages on bread and cartons of milk. It was our first introduction to hot dogs. We sat and stared through the window till it became dark. The train trip would last two nights and another day. We changed trains in Chicago, which became a blurry nightmare. Other passengers who had to do the same helped us get around. I remember being astonished at the friendliness and helpfulness of Americans. Coming out of a war where everyone only took care of himself, and during which people had become secretive and cruel, we had not expected such eagerness to help us from total strangers.

When our train finally pulled into the station at Lawrence, Kansas, Hank and I were extremely nervous. I secretly wondered why we ever undertook such an adventure. Full of anxiety, we gathered our belongings together and disembarked from the train. The moment we stepped onto the platform, flashbulbs started to pop in our faces, and we were surrounded by a large group of people. The Moorman family was there, and also people from the local newspaper. In triumph we were taken by taxi to their home on Mississippi Street. We had arrived! From Holland to America!

Fred and Hazel Moorman were in their forties. We met their son Bobby, my first pen pal, and their daughter Betty Jane, who also had been writing. Friends had been invited to meet us, and we learned firsthand how impossible it is to converse with people when you don't know the language. It felt very uncomfortable and unreal. Hank was totally stunned by the strange words directed his way, and I had my very first lesson in American conversation. I learned to distinguish the mumblers from the non-mumblers. The mumblers were people who talked fast and inarticulately, and whom I could not understand at all. The non-mumblers were those who spoke slowly and carefully, and I could understand them just a little.

We had our first American dinner in the kitchen, a large room with a large round table. I remember hot food, like potatoes and meat, and also bread and peanut butter. That was the strangest thing! Bread and potatoes at the same meal? We grew up either eating a hot meal without bread, or bread without anything hot. A memory flashed through my mind of the hot stew and the homemade bread I had eaten the time I ended up at Hank's home during the Hunger Winter.

After dinner was over and the dishes were washed, a big pan was set on the stove, and in it was poured some oil and then a big scoop of yellow corn. We looked at each other with questions in our eyes. Corn? We had not seen any chickens around, but they must have some at the back of the house. Then we wondered if they fried the corn first, before they fed it to the chickens. The lid was put on the pan, and soon we heard the loudest noises! There was a clattering of popping inside that pan. I became very worried, and expected the lid to blow off at any moment. When the lid did come off, the handful of yellow corn had become a mountain of fluffy white puffs! Hazel put some melted butter and salt on the "chicken feed," and then put it into bowls and handed one to each of us.

"Here," she said. "Have some popcorn."

Noticing how pleased she was, we realized that this was something we were supposed to eat. Not wanting to be impolite, we carefully tasted the popped corn and found that it tasted like...nothing. We did manage to eat it. It would take years before we liked popcorn, and Hank never really did.

We wanted to go to work immediately, because we had promised not to become a burden to our sponsors. Fred soon found us jobs in the Stokely Van Camp canning factory, on the late evening shift from six in the evening till two in the morning. Hank loaded railroad cars and I worked on a running band putting one piece of pork into each passing can. It was tedious, boring work. We walked home on freezing, snowy roads after work, because we did not have a car and the buses did not run that late. Was it only four years since the Hunger Winter in Holland? It was cold then, too, as I walked over icy roads wishing I were somewhere else. The only difference now was that we were not hungry.

So we were in America, working in a drafty factory, walking through zero-degree temperatures in the middle of the night. Hank also washed cars by day, from noon till five. I was not happy at all with our situation. Where were the beautiful, big houses? Where were the rich people with their automobiles? We had no friends, and no relatives nearby. Even unpleasant, hateful relatives started to look good during this time.

One night, plodding home, I complained to Hank, "I want to go back home. I don't like it here."

"Quit talking like that," he answered. "We wanted to come here. We are here, never look back. Only look forward."

That became Hank's motto in life—don't look back, just look forward.

Those first months in America were not easy. Fred and Hazel belonged to a club and spent every weekend there, only coming home to sleep. Kansas was dry at the time, no liquor being sold. Betty Jane's husband owned a lounge in Kansas City, Missouri, and he brought liquor in by the case. Fred, Hazel, and their friends would take it to the club and party from Friday night till Sunday night. We had to fend for ourselves during those times. Betty Jane lived in Kansas City and Bobby worked there also, only coming home occasionally. We were quite alone, and it was a lonely beginning of our new life.

Thirteen

THE AMERICAN DREAM did not turn out exactly as we had visualized it. Our immigration to America seemed such an adventure, such a wonderful and exciting thing to do. Those first months, the truth appeared to be a bit different, however. To leave one's country is like going through a painful divorce. You live a certain way all your life, either good or not so good. You live with the history of the place of your birth. You know all the national jokes, some dating back centuries. You sing the songs. You are familiar with all the old sayings, the idioms, the expressions that only the people of the land of your birth recognize and understand.

There are customs, like drinking tea for breakfast, having coffee at eleven o'clock in the morning, having tea again in the middle of the afternoon, and coffee at night at 8 o'clock. In good times food is delivered to the door. The butcher, the baker, the milkman, they all deliver. If they happen to come to the door at eleven in the morning, they are offered coffee. In the afternoon they may have tea. They will drink it standing at the door, and be off again to the next customer.

All these are seemingly unimportant habits and customs, but you grow up with them. Then there are the cities, the small, cozy villages, the many canals, the age-old cathedrals, cobbled streets, some dating from the time of the Romans. Pieces of walls built more than a thousand years ago to keep the Vikings out. It is a way of life; it was your life. And you leave all that.

You know the language you grew up with. You are secure because you are Dutch, and everyone you know is Dutch. You are used to certain kinds of food and the way it is cooked.

Then you land in America, the melting pot of many nationalities, a young, aggressive country only a few hundred years old. You have heard about "culture shock" and you know it exists—now you're living it.

Probably the most difficult of all is not understanding the new language. Language is so much part of a culture, of a nation's way of life. It is truly the mirror of the society in which people live. I have always marveled at Hank, who did not know one word of English when we arrived in America. He never complained about it or became frustrated. Instead, he threw himself into learning the American language. At work he was shown what to do, and he copied it. Amazingly, he picked up the spoken language quicker than I did, even with my four years of book-English. My proper English with the British pronunciation interfered with the colloquial language I heard around me.

Hank never shrank away from anything. He was indeed the leader of our family of two. I could never have lived through those first months without him there, as my friend and my husband. If possible, we grew even closer together, because the two of us were all we had in this world.

Language proved to be a stumbling block sometimes, but our lack of understanding could also be quite funny on occasion. One day a neighbor knocked at the Moorman's door early in the morning and announced quite excitedly that John, the man who lived across the street, had kicked the bucket. Hazel grabbed her chest and sat down, obviously upset by this pronouncement.

"How terrible!" she exclaimed. "I didn't know he was sick! What happened?"

I was confused and couldn't imagine how kicking a bucket could possibly make someone ill. It took me a while to understand that John had died during the night. Now, if she had said, "John blew the march of the crows," of course I would have known immediately what she meant.

One time, Hank attempted to describe the terrible storm we lived through while crossing the Atlantic and said, "We were shitting in our deck chairs when they tipped."

He meant that we were sitting, of course. We had never heard the other word he inadvertently used. We did think it odd at the time the way people were reacting to Hank's story, turning red and trying not to laugh. It was a long time later that we learned what he had said.

In early spring we experienced a climate shock. The temperatures in March soared to 85 degrees, and when we complained about the heat we were told that this was nothing, and just wait till summer when the temperatures rose to 100 or more. When I was a child going to school in Holland, the teachers sent us home whenever the temperature reached 80 because it was considered too hot to be in school. Used to our cool climate, Hank and I never really got used to the Kansas heat.

During March we heard about a job for Hank on a farm north of Lawrence. He was hired, and to our joy a house came with the job. With our earnings we bought our very first car, a 1936 dark blue Chevy, because we would be living in the country now and needed transportation to get around. We felt incredibly rich with our car! We had only been in America for a few months and we already had a car. I remember we paid $250 for that Chevy, and it was not in bad shape at all.

We thanked the Moormans for their hospitality and moved into our very first place of our own in America. The house was a big, square, two-story farmhouse without running water, just a pump in the kitchen attached to an old sink. The floors were plain wooden planks. A giant black monster of an old-fashioned cookstove stood in the kitchen and was the only means of heating and cooking. Next to an old garage stood something like a little shed called an "outhouse," with two open holes on the seat. It did have a door. We were warned about snakes frequenting the place. After we first saw that outhouse, my fantasies of big, elegantly furnished houses with curving staircases evaporated and I was forced to face reality. We had nothing, needed everything, and it was time to get to work creating a home for Hank and me. We had each other, and together we could overcome anything.

On the day Hank started working for the Beck family, I stayed behind in our new home and was quite content. Hank's earnings would be one hundred dollars a month and there was no rent to pay. A neighbor of the Moormans had given us an ancient iron bed with an old mattress. We bought a rickety kitchen table for three dollars and found three chairs in an alley in town, apparently thrown out. The Beck family gave us two pillows, some sheets, and blankets. In the dime-store in town we bought enough dishes, pots, and pans to get by. Some old cotton tablecloths served as temporary curtains. All in all, our new home didn't look too bad. A giant oak tree stood in front of the house, shading the front porch.

The Beck farm was large. It consisted of wheat fields, corn, potatoes, and beef cattle. Hank was a quick learner, and before long he could drive the tractor as if he was born to it. He still did not speak English—or American, rather—very fluently, but by being shown what to do he got by very well.

I worked at a hotel in town because we needed the extra money. I drove to work. Hank had taught me to drive and I had taken and passed the exam for my driver's license. Town was only three miles away, and I felt like a queen, driving my car. The hotel I worked at was a historic place. It was raided and burned by Quantrill's raiders during the Civil War and a large plaque on the front of the building reminded people of that event. I hated that job as much as the cannery, but I was not about to sit home when I could bring in a little extra cash.

That summer I quit the hotel and worked in the potato harvest in the grading shed. It was 100 degrees in the shade and we also experienced the Kansas humidity. We were always wet. Even after washing and changing clothes, we still dripped. The house did not have a bathroom, and the reluctant kitchen pump was very inadequate in hot weather. After the harvest, with the money I had earned we bought some things for our home: pretty, bright linoleum for our empty dining room, and a table and four chairs that were upholstered in red vinyl with a tulip design, which are still in the family more than half a century later.

For the living room we bought an old couch from a neighbor, covered with a light, floral slipcover, and a very cheap dark brown rug. We also found an old easy chair and purchased a tiny coffee table. A few of our old pictures were hung on the wall, and we felt quite proud of our first home in America. We had a garden, and Hank, brought up working in his father's garden, knew just what to do to grow vegetables. We also had apple and pear trees around the house. I loved country living, in spite of the many bugs and snakes. The copperheads and rattlers were especially frightening and dangerous.

I still had a lot to learn about American English. English is not a difficult language. The grammar is easier than most other languages, but the pronunciation is hard to master, because sometimes it makes no sense at all. One day a white truck pulled up to our house. I watched from the back porch and read these words: Manor House Bakery. I spelled it slowly in my mind: m-a-n-o-r, that's *manor*, with emphasis on the second syllable, pronouncing it like "manure." I bought a loaf of bread and some cinnamon rolls. I proudly told my neighbor that the Manor truck came to the house and I had bought some Manor bread. I thought it strange that she seemed embarrassed, but thought nothing of it. Later I told the wife of Hank's boss the same thing, and how nice it was that a Manor truck had stopped. Again I became aware of a suppressed giggle, but then she kindly and carefully told me that I pronounced Manor wrong, and what it really was that I was saying.

After the potato harvest we decided that I should find another job because we were very poor. The hundred dollars a month that Hank made didn't stretch very far. We barely made it from paycheck to paycheck, but prices were cheap. Gasoline was thirteen cents a gallon, for example. Twice a month we allowed ourselves to go to the movies. For 39 cents each we saw two main features, world news, and a cartoon. A bar of chocolate, divided between us, was 5 cents.

We were not unhappy. We just did with what we had. When there was no money, we didn't spend it. We bought groceries very carefully and nothing extra. Hank worked six days a week, from dawn till dusk, and our Sundays were spent sitting on the porch drinking iced tea. We were content for the time being. We knew we would not always live like that and we would have to build a future, but Hank and I were always good at doing with what we had, no matter how little. The one thing we were forced to purchase that summer, however, was a refrigerator. In the heat of a Kansas summer, food spoiled almost as quickly as we brought it home from the store. We didn't have money to buy such an expensive item, and we paid for it in installments. Growing up in a country where buying "on time" was a disgrace, we were horrified that we were forced to do this, but we had no choice. So our humble, shabby kitchen sported a gleaming, shiny white refrigerator. We were quite proud of it. But the best part of all was that we had each other. Experiencing this new life together proved to be a good thing.

The downside of all this was the loneliness we experienced. Even though we were together much of the time, we still missed friends. We didn't know anyone other than the people Hank worked with, and they paid no attention to us at all. We didn't go to church. Hank was not used to going to church because of the falling out his parents had with their local village church when he was growing up. So we didn't have fellowship that way, either. Hank's boss, Wilhelm Beck, did not attend church, although his family was Lutheran from way back. Once we did go to a little Baptist church, but the language of religion was so hard to understand that Hank decided we would not go back again.

Occasionally we visited the Moorman family. They had sponsored us, and we felt very grateful toward them. They were usually busy on the weekends and did not pay much attention to us.

The year came to an end, and we arrived at New Year's Eve, the last day of 1949. It was hard to imagine that only five years ago we were in the midst of the infamous Hunger Winter. I remembered eating tulip bulbs for dinner, shivering from the cold and fear, and that day I met Hank again after we had gotten to know each other as children. I remembered falling in love, and now here we were in our big, drafty house in the middle of Kansas, huddled near our black iron cookstove.

All that day I felt sad and a bit depressed. Even though I had not always been happy in Holland, I did have some good memories of New Year's Eve. During my childhood the entire family of my mother's—her parents, brothers and wives, and their children—would gather together in the evening. Oma and Opa baked the Dutch *oliebollen*, a kind of donut without a hole, that was leavened with beer and then deep fried in oil. Sprinkled with powdered sugar, the *oliebollen* were a New Year's Eve tradition. At midnight all the ships moored in the harbor of Rotterdam would sound their horns. An earsplitting explosion of sound, this concert would last for at least five minutes. After the noise died down again, one short, lonely blast followed. The entire family waited for that final toot, because that was our Uncle Cor, who usually had to be onboard his river barge and who, in spite of always getting into trouble for this, would have the last "word." And then our Queen Wilhelmina would speak on the radio, and name all the seamen and the names of ships that were on the oceans at that particular time, and wish them a Happy New Year.

Next, a long table was covered with a white sheet and the eating began: steaks and french fries, beer and gin for the grown-ups, and lemonade for the children. No one went to bed until the wee hours of the morning, except us children, who usually fell fast asleep right after the french fries.

Even though my childhood was never very happy, memories like our New Year's Eves still bring a smile to my heart.

It became time for me again to find a job. I was through with factories, hotels, and potato harvests and wanted to go back to what I had been trained for—secretarial work. I had a nice talk with a lady at the employment office, and after some hesitation she sent me to apply at a law office.

The lawyer who needed a secretary was friendly and quite young. He asked me if I knew shorthand. I told him yes, I knew shorthand in Dutch, but I would know English shorthand by Monday. That intrigued him so much that he told me I could start working after the weekend.

I went home wondering what I had gotten myself into! Knowing shorthand by Monday! I started thinking. There must be a way. The English alphabet was the same as the Dutch one. An *a* was an *a* in both languages, only it was pronounced differently. I took a piece of newspaper, paper, and pencil and started copying the words in shorthand. It worked! Using the Dutch marks for the English words was no problem at all, I thought. I could even read it back. Shorthand had shortcuts, and that presented a problem. I had to write the words down using every letter.

I practiced hard that weekend. I had Hank read to me while I tried to write it all down in shorthand. He read very slowly, of course, because he could hardly read English yet. On Monday morning I reported for work, my first office job in America! Soon I was called into the lawyer's office to take dictation. He started out briskly, and I became lost immediately. What language was this? I never heard these words before. I had to ask him to repeat several times, and when I finally sat down in front of the typewriter, I was shaking. It had never occurred to me that there existed such a thing as "legal" English. I struggled all morning with my first dictation. I had no trouble typing English, but what was I actually typing? I was determined to get better. The lawyer possessed amazing patience to put up with such a secretary. He allowed me to stumble and learn, and gradually I started doing a little bit better.

After two months, the partner in the business came home from military service. He was an older man and rather haughty. He took one look at me and fired me promptly. I did not present the accepted picture of a private secretary. My accent was still very pronounced and sometimes hard to understand. I did not dress fashionably because we did not have the money to buy nice clothes. I wore no makeup, and generally must have looked awkward and old country. At any rate, that was the end of my law office career.

I marched back to the employment office and told my sad story. I was sent to an interview at an insurance company, where I was immediately hired as a typist. No shorthand, thank goodness! I returned home, quite satisfied. I had lost a job and gained a job, all in one day. We would have my salary now and live a little bit better.

Our second year in America passed rather uneventfully. Hank worked hard as a hired man on the farm. His American English became better than mine. I still struggled with the "mumblers." My job at the insurance company went smoothly because I was very proficient in typing and spelling. People were kind and helpful. I learned to garden and we raised vegetables, and Hank taught me how to can the produce, which he had learned from his mother. We were very happy together. We had fallen in love during the Hunger Winter in his parents' kitchen, and if possible, we were more in love with every passing day. Hank did not foresee a future for us in the kind of job he had at present, a fact that worried him a bit. We both knew, however, that it was too early to make any plans for a change. What would we do? Where would we go?

A nice thing happened that summer! It did not begin too well, but the end became a great blessing to us. The farmer's son was getting married, and he wanted to build a house on the spot where our house stood. He wanted the shade trees that offered some coolness in the hot summers. Our humble house was moved into a cornfield, without any trees or shade. The outhouse was demolished and we had to do with the cornfield as bathroom, and haul in our water supply. That was a very hard and inconvenient time. But it all turned out for the good, however, because the farmer now decided to build a real bathroom in our house, a simple kitchen with real hot and cold running water, and he even installed an oil furnace in the basement. After all that, we even got fresh wallpaper, and they built a small garage. We had no big, shady trees anymore, but several new little ones were planted, and after everything was finished we felt happy with the many improvements.

In the spring of 1951, it started raining and raining. It rained for forty days until the levees could no longer hold back the water. The great Kaw River, or Kansas River, as it was also called, poured over the land. Hank and I had never experienced a flood, even coming from a rainy country far below sea level. There had been floods, of course, but not while we were living there.

It astonished us to see the water rising in the fields, covering the early crops, and continue rising. We had to leave our home, naturally. Before we evacuated, we took most of our belongings up to the second floor, and piled other things on top of our tables and a chest of drawers, not realizing that these wooden items would float and possibly tip over. Neighbors farther up the road who lived on higher ground offered to let us stay with them, and so we had a place to live for the time being. The flood covered a large area, as far as Kansas City, where lots of cattle penned up in the great stock yards drowned.

Our house ended up with five feet of water in it before the flood waters began to subside. When we were able to enter our home again, we discovered a mess! The brand new wallpaper had peeled off the walls, floors were buckled, and the basement was full of dirty, awful-smelling water. A strange-looking creature, something between a crab and a fish, was moving around in the bathtub.

The weather turned dreadfully hot after the flood, and the great clean-up began. It took a long time to get our house livable again because the houses of the farm family were cleaned up first. But when fall arrived, everything was in order once again, and we anticipated the next great event.

Back in Holland, Hank's sister Pat and her husband Tony Vangemeren, had also decided to immigrate to America to join us. They had two young children, Casey and Mary, and, being dissatisfied with life in postwar Holland, they decided to make the great move also. Hesitantly, we asked Fred and Hazel Moorman if they would perhaps like to sponsor Pat and Tony as well, and without having to think about it, they said they would.

In the middle of November that year, they arrived in Lawrence and lived with us for a short time. Tony also got a job on a farm, and as usual, a house went with it.

We now had relatives, and what a great feeling that was! We no longer were alone, and now we could visit and talk with people who spoke the same language.

At about that same time we acquired a lifelong friend, also a Tony—Tony Van Leiden, a Dutchman. He had come to America all by himself and found work on a farm run by Mennonites south of Lawrence. He heard about us and contacted us. He and Billie Jean, the girl he married, became our best friends. Our social life was expanding, we felt we were becoming more American, and were now quite at home in our new country.

Fourteen

THE GREATEST EVENT during those early years happened on November 4, 1952; Hank and I became parents! Our first baby was born, a little girl, Katherine Ann, called Kathy. She was born on the day Eisenhower was elected President of the United States. It took quite a while for the little lady to make her entrance into the world. When she finally emerged, I heard the nurse say, "Look at those eyelashes!" They were thick and dark, matching her dark hair, Hank's hair.

I said, "That's Hank!' She looked like him already.

After several days in the hospital, as was the custom at that time, we brought her home, excited and totally in love with our first offspring. I was learning to nurse her, and she seemed to be hungry all the time. When I had to feed her during the night, Hank got out of bed with me, sat next to me, handed me clean diapers, and declared, "She is my baby, too. We both take care of her, and both get up." And he did just that.

From the beginning he was a super dad.

I had become a mother now, and it changed me profoundly. I had brought into the world this perfect little human being, so helpless, so totally dependent upon me. The morning after I came home from the hospital and Hank had gone to work, I was alone with her for the first time. No crisply starched nurses, no admiring relatives hovering, we were completely alone. I was struck with wonder.

Her tiny naked body was lying on the bed, while I bent on my knees next to her. Fascinated, my eyes were glued to my brand new baby, our firstborn, this marvelous miracle made by us. I smelled the delicious, mildly scented baby soap, the fresh dab of powder rising from her minuscule bottom. Her eyelids, transparent and pearly like the inside of a shell, quivered, and she opened her eyes, staring at me in wonder. I carefully stroked the small head, feeling the downy dark hair. It was shaped with perfect bangs, as if especially styled that way.

My fingers traveled over the tiny cheeks. How could human skin be so soft, so satiny, and so perfect? Long, feathery lashes outlined curious eyes of an undetermined blue, that later would turn hazel.

I loved the feel of silk and velvet, but nothing equaled the skin of my baby. Round little arms of the most delicate pink were moving with amazing energy. Her hands, like tiny pillows, with microscopic fingers and perfect nails, seemed to want to grab something and I held out my finger. She latched on to it, and I imagined she had a surprised look on her darling face.

My eyes traveled down to her legs, sturdy and round, velvety soft, ending in ten tiny toes. I rose to my feet, picked her up, and hugged her against me. This wonder of creation was mine, ours, a gift from God. She whimpered and the thought occurred to me that I should dress and diaper her, and feed her. She started to make peeping noises, and the rosebud mouth was sucking.

The tiny cotton shirt was still too large for her. A clean diaper covered her velvety bottom. I wrapped the knit blanket snugly around her, hiding all the silkiness and tenderness of that incredible little body.

We sat together in the rocking chair, and I watched that hardworking, eager mouth with fascination. On that quiet, solitary morning, a lifelong love affair began as I was being transformed into that most special being—a mother.

An interesting story is connected with the birth of our first baby. At that time, having a baby cost two hundred and fifty dollars. That included the doctor, the prenatal care, five days in the hospital, and the follow-up care. We had been very worried about this large expense. We had not been able to save too much from our one hundred dollars a month. Some time before she was due, we received a letter from a lawyer in Holland with information that my grandmother on my father's side had died. It stated that according to Dutch law, I, her only grandchild, was to receive a very small part of the inheritance, even though she had tried to cut me out of her will entirely. The lawyer had found our address through emigration authorities, amazingly.

We signed a paper and returned it. One week before Kathy was born we received a check from Holland in the amount of two hundred and fifty-four American dollars, enough to pay the entire doctor's and hospital bill, with four dollars left over. It was one of those times that convinced us that God, as usual, had taken care of us.

To be parents, Hank and I discovered, cannot be taken lightly. We entered an entirely new phase of life. For seven years the two of us experienced the freedom to do anything we wanted to do. We witnessed the end of World War II, we married, and immigrated to a far away, different part of the world. We started working in new and sometimes difficult surroundings, but we always felt the two of us, together, could handle anything that came across our path.

Now we were responsible for this third person, who was totally dependent on us for love, food, warmth, and comfort. After all this time just being together, we suddenly became parents. The great love between us easily expanded to include our child. There was plenty to go around, an endless supply of love, never running out.

We loved being parents. Hank proved to be a superb father and family man. Never having known my own father and having missed him, I always thought if I ever had a husband he had to be a good father.

Hank never disappointed me. Our child became number one. Selfish wants and needs were discarded. Our first question always was, is this good for the baby?

After Kathy was born, Hank's boss came to see us. He told us something we never forgot: "Don't ever do to your child what my parents did to me. My parents came from Germany and never learned to speak English, therefore they never taught me either. I grew up speaking only German. When I started school I didn't know or understand any English at all, and it was the worst time of my life. I never fit in. Remember your child is an American, and treat her as such."

We realized that we spoke Dutch together and a bit of English to the baby. What Hank's boss told us made great sense. We threw out the Dutch right then and there, and spoke nothing but English from then on, to each other and to Kathy.

Pat and Tony did not agree with us, and continued speaking only Dutch. When their eldest, Casey, went to school he didn't know one word of English and had a very hard time.

Many events happened during our first five years in America. In 1953 Hank's brother Bas also came to the United States with his family. At about the same time the oldest sister, Cor, and husband, Hannes, and kids immigrated to Australia, the fourth one of the five Rosmolen siblings to leave their country of birth. Only Marie, the middle sister, remained in the Netherlands.

In the spring of 1954, Hank and I became citizens of the United States of America. We had studied hard to pass an examination testing our knowledge of the Constitution. That had not been easy, especially for Hank, who was not fluent in reading yet. On a hot, 100-degree day we went to Kansas City, and together with another group of people from diverse backgrounds were sworn in as American citizens. It was a great day for us! We already felt American for quite a while, to the distress of the relatives who declared we had become so different, not Dutch any longer. They did not mean this as a compliment, but we took it as such, and were very happy to hear it. We decided that in order to live in our adopted country, we could not hang on to being foreign and Dutch; we had to become Americans, also for our children's sake.

They were American born and would not want to be different from other children.

At about the same time we became citizens, we also discovered that a second baby was on the way. Hank, who had been thinking about the future for a while, became convinced that he could not remain a hired man on a farm all his life, and that it was time to try something else. We wanted to give our children a good life, a better one than we had known, and a hired man's wages were not exactly a comfortable living.

He started to search out jobs, and one day ended up in Topeka, Kansas, at the Goodyear Rubber and Tire Company, a vast complex with headquarters in Akron, Ohio. He went into the office of a very pleasant man for an interview, but was told that the hiring quota had just been filled and there were no more job openings. They talked a bit, and the man became very interested when he heard that Hank was born in Holland and lived there during the war.

He told Hank that during the war he had been a pilot and was shot down somewhere over Western Holland. His plane crashed in a field, but miraculously he escaped without a scratch. There were some young fellows close by who picked him up and took him in the darkness to a large barn. The barn held lots of hay bales, neatly stacked. The young men removed some of them to expose a sort of hideaway, complete with cot, chair, and vent for air. They deposited the pilot inside, and left, returning later with bread, cheese, and coffee. They also brought a small oil lamp and told him not to use it unless it was strictly necessary. The hiding place was closed off again with the hay bales, and he was left alone, wondering what would happen next. Days later he was transported at night to a place at the coast, where he stayed till the liberation.

As they talked about the details, Hank realized that he was probably one of the young men who had rescued and hidden this pilot. At some point the same thing occurred to the other man, and his face turned white as sheet. As Hank told it later, the two of them stared at each other in astonishment, both moved to tears. The man picked up his phone, quickly dialed a few numbers, and almost shouted into it, "Curly, we have another one...I *know*, but we're taking one more!" and slammed the phone down. Looking at Hank, he said, "Welcome to Goodyear!"

So, after five years on the farm, Hank went to work for Goodyear. We rented a large, old, rock house with a big garden plot for forty-five dollars a month, still in the same area, and Hank started to commute to Topeka in an old truck he bought. The farmer was quite angry that Hank quit, telling him that he had "picked us up from the gutter" and did not appreciate Hank leaving him. We were sorry that Mr. Beck felt that way, but the future beckoned, our future.

Hank started working for Goodyear on his thirty-first birthday, January 12, 1955. We settled into the rented house. It had a real bathroom, which we did not take for granted anymore, and there was a huge basement, dark and musty. I would even call it "spooky."

Hank was paid by the week. The first paycheck he came home with was displayed proudly on the kitchen table. We sat down next to each other, staring at it—ninety-eight dollars! We couldn't believe our eyes, ninety-eight dollars for one week's work. How rich we were! The rent for our big house was reasonable, gasoline and groceries were very cheap, and our finances looked a lot brighter.

In February our second child was born, our Janie. I fully expected a boy, because in wanting another girl so badly I felt I could not be that lucky twice. But here she was, another girl, our little Jane Christina. Hank was delighted too. He never even mentioned a boy. When asked, he would always say, "I would not trade any of my girls for a boy."

By now I was an old hand at mothering. Even so, I could not keep my eyes off this beautiful baby. She was so perfect, blond and fair, with the bluest eyes and the most delicate profile. She was a very good, satisfied baby who seldom cried, and giggled out loud at four weeks. I would stand long minutes by her bassinet, just staring at this tiny miracle. Where Kathy had been quite a fussy baby, Janie was serene. That was the perfect word to describe her. She was a big baby, nine pounds at birth, and twenty-two inches long.

The great love that dominated our lives since our eyes met in that warm kitchen during the Hunger Winter now enveloped four people. That is the marvelous thing about love—you never run out and there is always enough to go around.

Fifteen

THE GOODYEAR JOB lasted six years. Hank was a hard worker and a quick learner, which was recognized early, so after only nine months he was promoted to supervisor, with a large increase in salary. It was a hard job, especially in the summer, when the temperature climbed to over 100 degrees in the plant. Air conditioning did not exist in his area, and especially during day shift the heat was hard to bear. Being a supervisor, his shifts rotated every three months between day, evening, and night. The night shift was actually the worst, because he didn't get enough sleep during the day.

In spite of bad working conditions due to the black dust from the mixing of the rubber, which got into his lungs, he worked hard. He was determined to make a good living for his family. One year he even worked all through his two-week vacation instead of taking a much-deserved break.

When Janie was almost two years old, my mother came to visit for a three-month stay. To my deep regret I realized that we had nothing in common. My childhood, which I had tried so hard to forget, came back to me in many unhappy memories. Being a mother myself now, I saw with clarity how much she lacked the ability to love, even her own grandchildren. I was deeply aware of my resentment toward her, and unfortunately it was not till many years later that I was able to feel compassion for her, and to recognize that her life had not been easy either.

Janie, no matter how sweet and giggly she was, had a mind of her own, and up till then had refused to be toilet trained. Toilet training started very early in Holland; as soon as a child could walk, the potty chair was introduced. With Kathy it had been extremely easy. She thought it was a wonderful game to sit on her little chair. Janie was of a different opinion.

My mother was quite horrified, and considered that this whole situation showed my lack of skill as a mother. She decided to fix that. She took one of Janie's tiny training panties, bright yellow it was, and, after rummaging in my sewing box, found all kinds of colorful ribbons and scraps of material. Painstakingly she formed tiny ribbons and sewed them all over the panty.

"There now," she said to Janie, wagging her fingers with a frown. "Don't make it wet!"

Janie stared at her for a moment with her very blue eyes, giggled, and promptly wet her yellow, gaily be-ribboned panty. My mother, who had fully expected the problem to be solved, scolded her, but Janie left the proof of disobedience in a little heap on the floor, and ran around without, having great fun.

The day my mother left to return to Holland, Janie went to the bathroom, sat on the small potty chair, and acted like a little lady. I had followed her, and stared with amazement. She nodded at me with a very satisfied grin, and was completely toilet trained from that moment on.

Later that year, we bought our first house. After almost seven years in Kansas we had saved enough money for a down payment on a two-story house in the country, east of Lawrence. It stood on a hill with a beautiful, wide view over the countryside. We bought the house from an elderly couple who wanted to move to Mount Vernon, Washington, where their children lived. The payments were low, and we could well afford them. There was an elementary school nearby, and Kathy, although not quite six years old, was able to enroll.

With the house came a family of turkeys, three hens, and a very large, dignified tom. The girls quickly named him Grandpa. We had never been around turkeys before, but we discovered what fun they were. They would sit down right in front of our feet, wanting to be petted. After we would speak to them and pet them, they would wander off again.

We also now had a fishpond with real goldfish and, to our shock, a congregation of black widow spiders in the barn. The scariest of all, though, was the colony of aggressive wasps living in a giant oak tree, right near our mailbox.

We were proud of owning our first home, and enjoyed living there for a couple of years. The small storm cellar came in handy during those years because of the many tornado warnings we experienced. We never got used to those violent thunderstorms, the pounding rain, and the black funnel clouds that could develop unexpectedly. Neither Hank nor I were enchanted with Kansas. It had become home, of course, but we could not get used to the climate, especially the summers.

The other family members were all quite settled by now. Bas and Jo worked on a dairy farm and were planning to eventually buy one of their own. Tony worked as a mechanic for the Chevrolet dealer in town, while Pat got a job as a cook at the school where Kathy attended. They served hot lunches there every day.

The people Hank and I had bought our house from wrote, telling us how much they liked Washington. It was much cooler, it rained a lot, and was always green. We really liked that. It sounded like the climate in Holland.

"You don't suppose," Hank asked one day, "that it would be a lot nicer to live in Washington than in Kansas?"

"But what about jobs there?" We had two children now and were responsible for them first of all. It would not be so easy to start all over again somewhere else.

The thought, however, did not leave us. The work at Goodyear had taken its toll on Hank. I had become quite concerned about his lungs. He coughed often, and the phlegm would be streaked with black from the rubber dust he was working with and inhaling. It was even hard for him to be clean. After a shower his pores would still be embedded with black. It was a good job financially, but I felt that money was not the most important thing in life. He was always tired, did not sleep well, and was often quite grumpy.

It would not be an easy step to leave. It sounded like another emigration, traveling thousands of miles away from Kansas where we now had some relatives. Finding another job, a home; what were we thinking of?

It took us two years of weighing every aspect of another big move, but after I developed a bad case of hay fever and started to have asthma attacks, Hank decided it was time to move to Washington State.

We wrote to the couple we bought our house from, and they promptly invited us to stay with them till we could find a place of our own. The die was cast, and preparations began. We sold our home rather quickly, as well as some of the furniture, like the old piano we had been given by some neighbors. We studied maps and figured out a route to travel to the far Northwest. This time it would not be just the two of us, accompanied by two suitcases. We had children and accumulated stuff.

Just like eleven years before, when we informed our families that we were going to America, we encountered the same reactions when we told the relatives that we were going to the Northwest, to the state of Washington. We invited them to come along, but they declared that we were quite silly and strange, and predicted that it would all turn out to be a great disaster. Nevertheless we had made up our minds, and nothing could alter our decision.

❦

We left Kansas for Washington toward the end of March 1961. We had not given much thought to the fact that it was still winter in the mountain states. Kansas was so flat, with perhaps a few hills here and there. We had never traveled through the Rocky Mountains, and so we did not think about mountain passes or other obstacles that could challenge us.

The morning we left, we were sent off by all the relatives. Our caravan was quite a sight. Hank was in front, driving his old pickup truck loaded with furniture: the refrigerator, stove, beds, mattresses, and boxes. Towed by the pickup was a U-Haul trailer, also jam-packed with our belongings.

I drove behind him in our 1952 Buick packed with clothes and blankets. The Buick towed our fourteen-foot aluminum boat filled with boxes of tools, all kinds of odds and ends, and all secured with a heavy tarpaulin. Each of us had one of the girls next to us. They would change places often during the day. We had lunches, milk, and coffee with us, and after a tearful farewell from Pat, Tony, Bas, and Jo and the kids, we drove off. Tony and Bas followed us for at least twenty-five miles and then turned back. We were on our own again, once more heading for a totally new area, this time in the United States.

We had no idea what awaited us in Washington. In spite of a very uncertain future we were convinced of one thing—we could not continue living in Kansas. Hank could not work for Goodyear much longer for health reasons, and I was not much better off with my developing asthma. We needed fresh air, moderate temperatures, and green trees. We had made a good start in Kansas. We were Americans now, and we felt like the old pioneers heading west.

Hank never made a move without praying long and hard about it, and he was convinced that the Lord wanted us to go to Washington. With Hank feeling so secure about that, I was sure too. As always, I trusted him completely.

It was not an easy trip. Heavily loaded, we did not drive very fast, which caused angry honking from other drivers at times.

Janie, always prone to motion sickness, vomited several times, which caused delays when we pulled off the road to clean her up. We slept in motels at night and there was always that start again in the morning, promising another long day ahead of us.

The weather deteriorated. We came to icy, snowy roads and one time, while trying to cross a mountain pass, our truck could not take it. It kept sliding backward, and it became an anxious time.

A big semi-truck coming from the opposite direction came to a halt; the driver climbed out of the cab and walked over to our stalled truck. He was a skinny, very young man, shivering in a short jacket. He walked back to the semi and returned with a shovel. He started breaking up the ice under the pickup truck's wheels, and then hauled a small bag of sand out of his cab. He spread it in front of the wheels of our truck, all the while not saying one word. It seemed the most natural thing to help us. Hank pulled out his wallet, wanting to pay the man, but without a word he walked off, got into his truck and drove off, without so much as a wave.

We talked about it that evening in our motel. Hank wondered who that man was and where he had suddenly come from, and then decided that the Lord had sent him. Perhaps we were helped by an angel.

After seven days on the road we were all so tired, especially our two unhappy little girls, who had become quite bored just sitting in a vehicle all that time. We finally came to the state of Washington. Eastern Washington was still quite wintery and brown, with rolling hills as far as the eye could see, but once we crossed the Cascades, we were astounded! Everything was so green! The grass was thick and green, the trees were green, and we even saw tulips in yards. When we parked along a highway in the mountains, we smelled the air—so fresh and pure!

"Well," said Hank, "I guess this is the place for us to be!"

We found our way to Mount Vernon where the Kellers lived, called them from a phone booth, and at the end of the day were settled in their home, a log house near a lake.

We had done it! The big move had been accomplished. We had left Kansas behind, with so many memories of our struggles with new beginnings, and now were facing new struggles, once again vaguely wondering if we had done the right thing. One thing Hank and I never lacked, however, was courage. As long as we were together we were ready to tackle anything.

Being Dutch, the blood of mighty forefathers flowed through our veins. We came from a people who had sailed the vast oceans finding their way to the East Indies, the North Pole, and who, together with the British, destroyed the Spanish fleet centuries earlier. With the courage we had inherited from those old Romans and Vikings, plus a dose of stubbornness which helped us persevere, we would not easily give up in whatever we tried to do.

It took courage indeed to start all over again, but we had faith that we were being led by God, and like Hank always stated, we didn't look back.

Even if we didn't look back, it was hard to deny the backgrounds we had sprung from. My early years left permanent scars, emotionally and psychologically, and then the starvation during World War II caused some health issues I could not overcome. Hank did not experience the lack of food, but had gone through different kind of problems, like serving in the resistance, and living in hiding for over a year, and due to all of that, he missed out on an education.

So, brave and ambitious as we were, we were ready to start a new phase in our life, this time together with our Kathy and Janie.

PART III

Sixteen

~❦~

KANSAS WAS NOW in the past, like World War II and Holland, and we faced an entirely new life once again, this time in the state of Washington. Again we had no home, no job, no friends, and not even relatives. It was like the time we arrived in Kansas, but with two important differences: we spoke the language now, and we had two children.

After staying at the Kellers' for a couple of weeks, we rented an old house next to a little church. The house belonged to the church, and we were immediately invited to attend. As always, Hank was not inclined to go to church, due to the influence of his parents' unhappy experiences with the church in Woubrugge. He could not live without faith in Jesus, but organized religion was another matter. He did not want any part of it. I started to have a strong desire to belong to a church and to learn more about God, but we didn't go, of course.

This little church became instrumental in Hank's finding his first job in Washington. The first, the only, and the last. He was hired by one of the church members to work for his small manufacturing company. They made wire chicken cages for the large egg producers in the area. Hank started in at the bottom, learning to be a welder.

It proved to be a good, steady job, and he became quite interested in it. During his entire life, whenever Hank did something, he did it better than anyone else and would throw himself fully into whatever he chose to do at the time. The job became a challenge. The business needed to expand and grow, and the owner asked Hank to become the sales representative for the company. Originally just manufacturing cages for laying hens, the company added feeders and watering equipment, and a way was invented to remove the droppings from under the cages, which hung above the ground. Hank started to design different cages, and before long was drawing up professional-looking blueprints.

He was able to find customers all over Washington, and even into Oregon and Idaho. Sometimes he found business as far away as Montana and California. The business was growing by leaps and bounds. Hank was honest, reliable, and never pushy, and he became well liked among the poultry growers.

I didn't like his traveling at all. Sometimes he had to be away from home overnight, of course, and I became intensely lonely. To my astonishment I discovered that I was homesick for Kansas! Truly homesick! We had made a home there, settled down, had friends and family, and here we were, all alone once again. Hank met people through his work, but being a homemaker, I didn't get to meet anybody.

I missed the friendliness of the Kansas people. People were different in Washington, I thought, standoffish, and uninterested. Loneliness engulfed me, and I was profoundly unhappy. By not going to church, we didn't have fellowship with others. We didn't belong to the partying, drinking crowd either. We clung to each other, the four of us, and for the time being that was it.

On Sundays we explored. We discovered the beauties of our new area. I will never forget the excitement we felt when we discovered Deception Pass and stood on the bridge holding on to each other.

By that time we had bought a house, a big, old, two-story house on two-and-a-half acres at the edge of town. The price was nine thousand dollars, and the monthly payments were sixty dollars. We bought a few pieces of furniture, and combined with the things we had brought from Kansas, it looked very nice. A bit empty, but nice. After our Sunday drives it felt good to come home again to a place of our own.

In the fall we investigated the forests along the Skagit River, finding several parks and lakes. It seemed there was no end to our discoveries.

Winter approached, and I said to Hank one day, "I'm bored, and you are gone so much, I want to do something with myself."

He thought a moment. "Why don't you find a job?"

"What kind of job?"

"Just what you always have done, office work."

Then a light seemed to go on in his eyes, and he suggested, "Why don't you go to college?"

"College?" I was stunned. "And what would I do in college? I am almost thirty-seven years old."

"Just think a minute." He was all excited now. "When the girls are ready for college we are going to need lots of money. If you would become a teacher or something like that, we would be able to take care of their education."

I digested that for a while.

"But I am too old to go to college."

Hank was not to be put off that easily. He always thought about the future, always saw chances for improving life and moving ahead.

"Go find out," he finally said.

I pondered that suggestion for quite a while. Indeed, I had sometimes thought that I would like to be a teacher. I was very good at languages—I could teach French and German, for instance. But how could I go to college? I only had four years of high-school education, and that was twenty years ago. In Holland we had six years of elementary schooling, and then straight to high school. There were no middle schools. In our big-city schools, when we reached the fifth grade we had to take a state examination which determined what high school we would be able to attend. I was informed that I would be able to attend the four-year high school. If I had been smarter I would have been allowed to enter the five-year high school, or, if I was college material I could go to the six-year high school, which prepared for college. So actually, I went to the simplest school, which did not allow you entry into the university. We learned three foreign languages, English, French, and German, not as a choice but as a requirement. We did not choose our subjects; we were told what to learn. We also learned world history, world literature, geography, algebra, a little science, and gymnastics. That was the school for "dummies." So the prospect of being admitted to an American college was a bit daunting. I was sure they would have no part of me.

I met with a counselor at Skagit Valley College. I did not even have my high school diploma records, which were destroyed after the school was bombed during the war years. To my immense surprise, I was admitted to the college and received a list of the classes I would have to take. Because I had studied French and German for several years, even though that was so many years ago, I could not enroll in the first-year language classes, but had to take the second-year classes.

After Christmas, in January 1962, I started college. Kathy and Janie went to Washington Elementary School, and I had my classes arranged so that I left after they did, and I was home again before the bus dropped them off. They hardly knew I was gone.

So here I was, a college student. I was nervous and felt very conspicuous. I was 37 and in school again, with 18- and 19-year-olds. There were very few older students in those days.

My very first class was a world history class. I sat in front, not wanting to miss anything. We were told we had to write a term paper that quarter. What was a term paper? I had never heard the word and didn't know what to do about it. The instructor began lecturing about a man named Erasmus. Apparently he had written something important. It dawned on me that Erasmus was Dutch, and I suddenly remembered the gray stone statue in the park in front of my elementary school. I thought, is she talking about *that* Erasmus? Was he famous, or something? German and French classes seemed to be very easy, and I discovered to my surprise that I had forgotten very little from my high-school years.

Our lives took on a new direction. Hank worked hard at his job. The girls were adjusting to their school and seemed quite happy. I went to college and reorganized our lives accordingly.

Hank was an enormous help to me. He tried to be home earlier at night and helped with the dishes and chores around the house. Many evenings found the four of us sitting around our big dining room table, Hank with paperwork, I doing homework, and the girls either doing their homework or coloring in their color books. That was the big thing in those years, coloring books. There were no computers or video games. We had about ten channels of black-and-white television, of course, but with few programs they liked. On Saturdays Hank helped clean house, shop, and even do laundry. My college years became a true family affair.

After I finished Skagit Valley College we moved into town to a nicer home close to schools, and the following two years I commuted to Western Washington State College in Bellingham, where I graduated with a degree in secondary education, teaching French and German. After graduation I found a job teaching French and German at a high school in Marysville, south of Mount Vernon.

Hank, in the meantime, had made quite a name for himself in the field of egg producing and poultry equipment, and had become a partner in the company.

Our busy lives continued, and we were quite content. Every night we all had dinner together and talked about what happened to us during the day. On Sundays we still explored the countryside around Mount Vernon. That had become our favorite activity. We visited Seattle, the San Juan Islands, enjoying this family time, which to us was so precious.

We felt life was good, and were blissfully unaware, that problems were just around the bend. The turbulence of the 1960s coincided with the girls' reaching their teenage years. Hank and I had always naively assumed that our children would grow up to be carbon copies of us. We experienced a rude awakening when we were confronted with a period of rebellion and serious opposition to our way of life. Both of us had been raised by strict parents, and we followed that example, although we loved our children more deeply than we had ever been loved. Anxiety, tension, and vague fears became more common in our day-to-day lives. We did not understand what was happening and tried to figure out how to stop these changes in our once peaceful home.

Of course, the same situation was happening to many parents all over the country. We had arrived at the era of the hippies. It seemed a bizarre time to us. The crazier and messier teenagers were dressed, the more they were "with it." We were frightened when we started hearing and reading about mind-altering drugs. We only knew that drugs were prescribed by a doctor and purchased at the pharmacy when someone was sick.

During this period we cried out to the Lord to hold our children in His arms, and to let no harm come to them. More than ever we made sure our daughters knew we loved them unconditionally, no matter what. As they matured, life calmed a bit and we felt that God had answered our prayers.

To all our problems I added another one; I discovered that after going to college all these years, I did not like teaching! I had expected the teaching to be the same as I remembered in my Dutch high school, the students obedient and respectful, doing their homework without any protests. Instead, I was confronted by 150 students a day, in five different periods, the majority of whom didn't enjoy learning foreign languages and who were disrespectful, noisy, and lazy.

The principal was young and did not appreciate my handling of the students. I was strict and taught like I had been taught myself those many years ago. Of course, this did not work in the present society. My initial joy in presenting foreign languages to these young people disappeared, and instead I felt a great burden pressing down on my spirit. My enthusiasm left me, and I dreaded each day I had to drive to Marysville. Deep in my heart the knowledge that I did not like teaching nagged at me. I felt terribly bad about all this because Hank had so cheerfully sent me through college, committed to making the necessary sacrifices of money and time that could have been spent differently.

The second year was worse than the first one. The kids were becoming more unruly, and it became clear that some of them were under the influence of drugs when they were in class. Upon reporting this to the principal, I was laughed at, and I became the butt of all jokes among the other teachers. I was ready to throw in the towel.

One Friday evening, after returning from Marysville, I drove to a little dress shop in Mount Vernon to purchase some pantyhose. The owner was an older woman who confided in me that she was tired of working and wanted to sell her shop. She knew me quite well, since I bought many clothes there.

On the way home, I was thinking that I would love to have a dress shop of my own, and go into business.

The next morning I entered the bathroom while Hank was shaving.

"What would you say," I asked him, "if I told you that I would like to buy a dress shop?"

He turned his soapy face toward me. "What are you talking about?" he wanted to know.

"I want to quit teaching," I said hesitantly.

He was washing his face now, and mumbled something. Then he turned toward me and smiled.

"I've known that for quite a while," he said, "but is it not a little crazy to want to buy a dress shop? What about all those college years and all the effort you put into that?"

"I know. It sounds awfully silly."

I decided to drop the subject, but the thought kept playing through my mind. I visited the store again, and asked the owner how much she wanted for the business. She did not own the building, just rented it by the month, and did not even have a lease. I casually told Hank what I had learned from her about the business. She would sell it cheap, because she wanted to retire as soon as possible. In the meantime, I kept teaching and commuting every day, but my heart was not in it. I knew that teaching was not meant for me.

It never took long for Hank and me to make a decision, no matter how big or small. There were many differences between us, but when it came to really important things our minds operated as one. We were a tight unit, wanting the same out of life, which kept us together so closely all those many years.

We purchased the dress shop, known as May Johnson's. We paid a reasonable price, with not much of a down payment, and made small monthly payments. Rent for the building was only $250 per month.

I resigned from my teaching position, and after the fall semester of my second year of teaching it was over. A big load lifted from my shoulders, and I was ready to start the next adventure, the fashion business!

I remembered my years as a young girl, and also the war years. I usually owned only one dress and one pair of shoes. Often, even before the war, the soles of my shoes had holes in them, and I had to wear them till they literally fell apart. When I outgrew a dress, my mother cut it open down the middle and added a piece of fabric, often not even matching, and I would have to wear it like that. With my height and thick red hair (not admired in Holland), I felt very inferior to the smaller, well-dressed girls. Sometimes in my dreams I entered a room with a bed in it. On the bed I saw a suitcase. I opened it, and found it full of pretty clothes, all for me. The dream usually ended there, and I would wake up empty and sad.

It seemed unreal to own a shop now, full of pretty clothes. Hank still worked for the poultry business, so the store would be my department. I was totally without any experience. I had never sold anything or run a cash register, never dealt with customers, and knew absolutely nothing about the retail world. It was scary indeed, but I remembered how I had taught myself English shorthand, had finished college, and had survived World War II. With Hank at my side I could tackle anything. Whenever I faced something new in my life, something I really *had* to do, I figuratively closed my eyes and jumped right into it. That is what happened now. I had wanted a dress shop—*now work in it,* I told myself.

Hank and I had also thought that having a dress shop in the family would be good for our daughters. They could work in it after school and have a part in it. That did not work out as planned, but in the meantime I had to learn the business myself.

The first Monday morning when I unlocked the door to the store, I fully expected the former owner to be there, as promised. Apparently she changed her mind and did not show up. The one sales lady who worked there, and who we retained, had her day off. So there I stood, alone in the silent store, staring all around me, not knowing where to begin.

It proved to be an unforgettable day! Customers started coming in early, followed by many more throughout the day. Two salesmen showed up, trying to sell me blouses and dresses. The hectic activities prevented me from having time to eat lunch, and I could barely attend to the calls of nature! I felt worn out that night but experienced a profound feeling of satisfaction. I was my own boss! I would make a success of this business.

The first years became a season of learning, and did we learn! Hank took a lively interest in the business, besides tending to his own work, and accompanied me to all the markets. Several times a year salesmen from New York, Los Angeles, San Francisco, and Dallas descended upon Seattle to the Trade Center, and there we purchased merchandise. This was an education in itself. Some of the people were nice, but most were pushy, overly "sophisticated," contemptuous when they thought you were hesitating, and could be quite sarcastic when we didn't like a certain line of clothes. It seemed a perpetual fight to purchase what we knew we could sell, in spite of what they had in mind. It was good we were together in this endeavor. With Hank there beside me I had some clout.

There was one salesman from Los Angeles who seemed to like us. He sold a marvelous line of separates and kept it for our store exclusively, an unheard of event, which put us on the map. In the meantime we had changed the name of the store from May Johnson's to Fashions by Christina, which became a name well known at the markets and around town.

Our little business grew fast the first years. We bought another store, including the building this time, in downtown Mount Vernon and added a bridal shop on the second floor there. Then we bought an existing children's store, hired more salespeople, and I got busier and busier. I did all the merchandising, window decorating, bookkeeping and buying as well as putting on occasional fashions shows from Bellingham to Everett, and places in between.

While our business life thrived, our family life was far from ideal. To our great distress Kathy married one of her suitors. We knew this was a mistake and that the marriage was doomed from the beginning. But as always, we kept loving her and helping and emotionally supporting her. A baby boy was born out of this union, and to our great joy we were grandparents for the first time.

We found out once more that love will never be used up, that there is always plenty more where it came from. So we both fell in love with this little bit of humanity, this healthy, dark-haired grandson who laughed out loud at the age of four weeks. His name was Erik, and as the very first of the third generation, he became the symbol of the continuation of our family. As we held him in our arms, we hoped and prayed that his life would be easy and that he would never have to go through a war or hard times.

For Hank, little Erik became "his boy," and his delight knew no end.

One and a half years later Janie got married, also to a fellow who had disaster written all over him. We were also against that marriage, and I believed that this was belated rebellion from Janie, choosing someone so different from us. We were proved right, and she left him after a year and a half. He was emotionally abusive, and he reminded me strongly of my stepfather, with his hateful remarks, purposely humiliating her. Shortly after the marriage he got a job in Richland, and moving our daughter over there was the hardest thing we ever did. As we drove off, leaving her behind in that city across the mountains, I sobbed my heart out, and Hank for once did not tell me to stop. His eyes were wet too.

Seventeen

KATHY AND JANIE were married, and Hank and I were alone again. We were both busy, Hank with the poultry business in which he was now part owner, and I with three stores to run. We had a nice home and had even bought a small motor home, and apart from the worries about our children, we had a pretty good life.

At this time I became aware that I was not happy at all. Something seemed to be missing. I often felt cross and empty, and I could not figure out what was the matter with me. Hank loved me; I loved him. We loved to be together more than anything in the world. So why was I so dissatisfied? We still didn't go to church. Our Sundays were quite precious to us. We would take Hank's old pickup truck, make a bottle of coffee, grab the cookie tin, and set out for the hills in the mornings. We parked at some especially pretty spot, drank our coffee, and talked about the Lord. That was Hank's favorite subject. We felt so cozy and happy, and our conversations were like balm to the soul. Every Sunday morning we found a different spot, and we looked forward to this all week. But somehow even that did not seem to be enough for me.

A friend asked me in the fall if I would like to join her in a Bible study called Coffee Break. Everyone was welcome. It was at a church every Tuesday morning.

"No way," I answered. "I'm much too busy."

Imagine, I thought, *How can I do a thing like that?*

A whole year passed, and I didn't feel any better. Even Hank expressed the opinion that I was becoming a grouch.

Fall rolled around again, and the same friend asked the same question, "How about joining me in that Bible study at the church?"

I gave the same answer, "No way! How can I? I'm too busy."

The next Tuesday morning I got ready to go to the stores, all dressed up for work. As the car rolled down Division Street, I suddenly made a turn to the left. I had not planned anything, but within minutes I found myself parked in front of the church where my friend attended Coffee Break.

I felt bewildered. What was I doing here? Work waited at the stores. I was a busy woman. I sat quietly for a while. I had been wondering lately if I really was a Christian. I had lived with Hank all these years, listened to his talk about Christ, believed everything he told me, but often I felt like I was not sure what it was all about. Was I a Christian, a believer, or not? I read the Bible sometimes but it didn't mean a whole lot, since I didn't understand it very much. I truly believe at that particular time God was getting tired of me sitting on the fence and decided to give me a powerful push.

Not knowing what I was really doing, like being in a trance, I got out of the car and entered the church. I heard many voices of women. A lady met me at the door and smiled and shook hands. I heard myself say, "I have come for the Bible studies."

In minutes I found myself in a small room around a table with eight other women, none of whom I knew. I was handed a Bible, since I had not brought one, and was told we were in chapter two in the book of Acts. Clumsily I found it. Someone started to read. My heart was pounding. I listened. Suddenly a few words entered my brain, "All of them were filled with the Holy Spirit…"

I thought, *How can people be filled with the Holy Spirit?* Intently I listened, and it appeared to me like shells were falling from my eyes. Of course! The Holy Spirit has to make everything clear, in order for me to understand God, Jesus Christ, and the Holy Scriptures. Excitement mounted deep within me.

I promised to be back next week, and I went to work that day in a daze. In the evening, after dinner, I told Hank what had happened that day and that I was going to read the entire Bible. He seemed surprised, to put it mildly. And I started reading. That winter I read the entire Bible, seldom skipping a day. For the very first time I really understood! My restlessness, my feeling of discontent, my strange unhappiness, it all disappeared. The hole in my soul was filled with the love of Christ. I had many questions to ask of Hank, and our Sunday mornings in the hills became even more precious.

I changed. I started loving people, where I had not loved them before. A friend told me hesitatingly one day, "Christina, you are different. You are much nicer."

That gave me a jolt. I had thought I was pretty nice before!

The world seemed bathed in a soft glow. It reminded me of the time during the Hunger Winter in World War II, when life was at its darkest and I had fallen in love with Hank. I never forgot that glorious time, when I forgot all the miseries of the day and when I was truly happy for the first time in my life.

I had fallen in love again, this time with Jesus Christ, and the love for Hank, for my children, for relatives even, seemed multiplied. It was a new world for me. For the first time I genuinely knew that I was a Christian, a born-again Christian.

Now I understood that God loved me long before I knew Him. Incidents in my life jumped out at me! At three or four years old, despite living with anti-religious people, I had known that there was a God, a kind old gentleman dressed in white who floated over me. I remembered the war years. I experienced heavy bombardments but was never hit. I remembered the incident of the train crossing the Waal River. I had missed that train on my way home. That was the time an Allied plane dove out of the clouds and attacked it. Many people were wounded and even died. I even remembered the time I had angrily stuck out my tongue at a German soldier, who then started to follow me in the half-dark of the narrow street. He never caught up with me.

Above all, God brought me a Christian husband who set me on the road to find Him. I also learned now that another person cannot truly save you. You have to come to Christ all by yourself. You have to give yourself to Him. You have to accept Him by faith, your own faith, not someone else's, no matter how much that person loves you. God made clear to me that every person has to make his or her own decision, to accept that Jesus died on the cross for our own salvation, or to reject and disbelieve in His sacrifice. I accepted. No matter what happened in our lives, that certainty and joy would live forever within me.

I faithfully attended the Bible studies that year, never skipping, in spite of my heavy workload.

Work continued, and major events kept happening. Janie came home after leaving her husband for good, and tried to make a new life for herself. Kathy had twins, our Becky and Ian. If that wasn't something! A tiny boy and a tiny girl, beautiful babies, both of them.

Kathy's marriage was in trouble too, and our hearts ached because we knew how she tried to keep things together. Her husband had a passion for chasing other women, which became an intolerable situation. Instead of paying attention to Kathy and the kids, he lavished attention on whomever took his fancy. We knew this would eventually end in divorce, and it did.

Janie married again. Her husband was as fine a fellow as could be found anywhere. David became like our own son, and we loved him from the start. He was a decent and hardworking fellow, and we heaved a sigh of relief. This marriage lightened our load of worries considerably.

Around that time a great event took place—our family reunion!

Hank's sister Marie and husband, Henk, from Holland decided to take a trip to America and visit all the relatives. Hank's siblings were spread out all over the world. The oldest sister, Cor, (short for Cornelia) and husband, Hannes, lived in Australia. Sister Pat and husband Tony had stayed in Kansas, and brother Bas and wife Johanna lived in Missouri on their farm.

It was decided that they would all travel to Washington and stay with Hank and me, and so it happened. For three weeks all ten adults lived together in our home.

I had cooked ahead and our freezer was filled with food: roasts, meatballs, a turkey, pies, cookies, and cakes. I had been cooking and baking every spare moment. We had a big dining room, permanently set for ten people. Conversations during our meals were a challenge we never could have foreseen. The people from Holland did not speak one word of English. The Australians had learned the Aussie way of speaking English, and we could hardly understand them. Pat and Tony never learned proper English and spoke half Dutch and half broken English. Bas and Jo talked English fine, with a Midwestern drawl. I didn't know about Hank and me; it is hard to judge yourself. Henk and Marie acted furious whenever we fell into speaking English. I usually noticed that quickly. I would mumble across the table, "Speak Dutch, speak Dutch." The trouble was that some of us, especially my Hank, had forgotten most of their Dutch!

Hank and I had expected that we would have a lovely time together. Some of the couples had not seen each other for thirty years. Instead of that, there were many tensions, totally unexpected. Hank still had his work. I ran three stores. Sometimes it was hard to leave in the morning, and we hoped that the family would have a great time together in our absence.

We did a lot of sightseeing, of course. Hank and I took many days off or worked just a few hours. Sometimes it appeared to be pure chaos, but we had great times too. Just to see everyone together was a rare event. It would never happen again, and by all human reckoning it could be the last time we saw the Dutch and Australian relatives.

For the first time, I looked upon Hank's siblings through the eyes of the Lord. I felt a genuine love for all of them, the love of Jesus. I was able to peacefully handle any small or large problems that occurred, without getting mad like I would have done before I became a true Christian. Hank noticed this, and one evening, alone in our bedroom he took me in his arms and said, "I noticed how you are handling everything, and how nice you are. Thank you for being you."

Nevertheless, I rejoiced when the reunion ended. It left me overwhelmed and exhausted. Hank and I could again relax and just cater to each other and our family.

Our sighs of relief were soon changed into sighs of distress, however, when Kathy announced she was marrying again. She hardly knew this man, but he had zoomed in on her like a comet. He had two boys he would add to the family. When we met him, our hearts sank, and we foresaw another disaster. The boys he brought into the home had experienced a very dysfunctional childhood and caused all kinds of problems. The household sank into a never-ending mire of unhappiness and distress. Our children's and grandchildren's troubles always became our troubles, and Hank and I lost our peaceful lives again, for a time.

To top this all off, we received an unexpected letter from my sister Cora that she and her husband were planning a trip to the United States, and that they wanted to spend a couple of weeks with us. I had not seen Cora since Hank and I left Holland, and we never corresponded. Naturally I wrote back that they were welcome. I wondered how she had grown up, what kind of a person she would be.

Cora and her husband, Sybe, were two intellectuals immersed in writing and translating books. Sybe was a famous author whose books were required reading at the Dutch universities. Cora translated novels and movie subtitles out of Swedish into the Dutch language.

When they entered our home, I felt a moment of panic. It seemed as though a black cloud entered with them. Never had I experienced anything like that. I suddenly felt a vague fear and wished fervently that they had not come into our home. It soon became apparent why I had this unusual and strange feeling. They were both anti-Christian. Cora had clung to our upbringing, and Sybe was even more violently against anything religious. At our first meal together, when Hank asked God's blessing, they both sat back from the table, arms crossed, with raised eyebrows, and definite smirks on their faces. Later that evening Cora told me they simply could not understand how I, after being brought up the way I had been, could be so stupid as to fall for something like that. She thought what had happened to me was simply unbelievable. She shocked me so much that I was tongue-tied before her vicious criticism. When I told Hank, he said to not worry about this, because talking to them would be like throwing pearls to swine. He felt their darkness too, but not as deeply as I.

To my enormous relief they did not stay very long with us. And when they left, the dark spirit I so keenly perceived around them left too. As a Christian I had been oppressed by the presence of the ungodly, who could only be Satan. I resolved right then that never would I let them come into my home again, and I never did.

⊂∞⊃

The turbulent year of 1981 came to an end. I worked hard on the holiday season, the after-Christmas sales, and the family gatherings, and on New Year's Eve I said to Hank, "That was quite a year. Let's hope the next one will be a lot easier."

"You said it," he answered, comfortably stretched out in his easy chair. "I can do with some peace and quiet for a change."

We still had Kathy and the three grandkids to worry about, but Janie was happy with David, and we were sure things would be better, praying that the Lord would help our family.

We totally adored our grandchildren. They were often at our house, especially for overnight parties. Hank bought them all their first tricycles, and then small bicycles. The five of us went bike riding frequently, Hank in the front, the children in the middle, and me bringing up the rear. We often went as far as the park. Traffic was not too bad then. We lived on Division at that time, and took the side roads to the park. Even with all the hectic living, the unexpected events and visits from family, our three little kids always came first, and we felt rich with them. Our only regret for them was that they had a stepfather who did not know how to be a good dad. But they had a good mother, and that soothed our pain.

Eighteen

FOUR WEEKS INTO the new year, disaster struck. Kathy was working part-time in the stores at that time, and I told her one morning, "Kathy, if I ever get sick, you will have to do the payroll all by yourself, so let's do it together today, and you make notes so you will be able to handle it."

We sat together working all morning, but I had a strange sensation of not feeling well. I felt shivers going down my spine, as if I had a fever. I had a hard time finishing my work that day, and by evening I felt really sick. For two weeks I ran a fever of 103 and sometimes 104, totally unresponsive to antibiotics.

Then, on a Sunday evening I fainted, and when I came to, I could not use my left arm. Our good old doctor came immediately to our home and ordered me to the hospital in Sedro Woolley. After a few days, with all kinds of doctors hovering about me, it was discovered I had an abscess in the brain. I was wheeled into a small room, with Hank by my side, and we were shown a series of CT scan pictures which showed a bright blob on the ride side in my head. I had to be operated on as soon as possible, and the only place for that was Virginia Mason Hospital in Seattle.

When Hank left me that evening to go home, he was stopped by a police officer in the middle of Burlington for speeding. The officer realized Hank was crying and asked what was going on. Hank told him about my circumstances and sobbed even harder. The sympathetic officer let him go, after telling him that he would be praying for him and me.

Upon my arrival the next day at Virginia Mason Hospital, the doctors were waiting for me. The neurosurgeon told us that there was only a ten-percent chance of survival in a case like mine. I was too sick to even worry about that. Almost immediately I was taken into surgery, where I was told they could not give me any anesthetic, because they did not know what it would do to me.

The surgeon started to drill into my skull, and I was fully conscious, hearing everything that was going on. The abscess was drained, and some of the fluid spilled on the floor. I heard the surgeon holler at the nurses that he wanted the whole place cleaned up with antiseptic, thoroughly, and on the double!

When I was wheeled into the hall, Hank stood there anxiously waiting. I was amazed that I could lift my left arm again, and surprised Hank as I showed him.

Lab tests determined that I had a streptococcus infection in the brain, and the only medication that would get rid of it would be penicillin. It would have to be administered intravenously, day and night, in the hospital. Hank left for home without me, not knowing when I could come home again.

Ten days later I was told that the doctors were worried about a large shadow in my lungs and I would have to undergo a test. This twenty-minute test was the worst thing that ever happened to me in my entire life. I sat on a table, expecting to have another X-ray taken, or something like that. But instead, a narrow tube with a tiny camera attached to it was shoved up my nose, down my throat, and into my lungs. I choked constantly as the tube moved around in my lungs, taking pictures. It was horrible!

Back in my bed in my room I was crying hysterically. I told myself that it was not possible that God existed, because if He was real, He would not let anything like that happen to me.

Then it happened. I sensed in the corner of my room a very black shadow hovering, something threatening and downright scary. I sat straight up and stared. In a flash of insight I knew that the devil hovered in that corner, trying to get my soul away from God.

I became very angry and shouted, "Get away from me, you devil! I belong to Jesus!" The black presence disappeared in an instant, and I knew my heavenly Father was with me all the way, in spite of my moment of doubt.

The next day I underwent surgery on my lungs, which were filled with the same infection that had been drained out of my brain. How I got this infection was a puzzle to the doctors. Perhaps it was "walking pneumonia," but no one knew for sure. I later learned that several of the nurses were convinced I would die, and each morning I surprised them when they saw I was still alive.

Altogether I was hospitalized for two months, six weeks of these at Virginia Mason Hospital. The penicillin infusions continued throughout the days and nights. My veins corroded from the constant flow of drugs and it became harder and harder for the nurses to find a spot to insert the IV needle. One night it was really bad, and the attending nurse finally gave up. She left to get help.

I sat there in bed, leaning against the pillows. It was very quiet in the hall. No one was around. I felt utterly deserted and tears started spilling down over my cheeks.

I took my Bible from the nightstand and opened it at random. I read, "Do not fear, for I am with you, do not be dismayed, for I am your God. I will strengthen you and help you; I will uphold you with my righteous right hand" (Isaiah 41:10).

At that point a short, dark-skinned nurse entered and informed me, "I am an expert and I will get that needle in."

She slapped my arm, wrapped it in a hot towel, and left. I stared at the open door. After a short while she returned, removed the towel, and slid the needle into a vein without any problem or pain. She attached the penicillin bottle and off she went, all without saying another word—she was merely a shadow in a dim room. I never saw that particular nurse again, but that one time in the middle of the night she came miraculously to my rescue.

Slowly, oh so slowly, I recovered. I became a famous case throughout the hospital. One doctor told me the only brain abscess he had ever seen was during an autopsy. The surgeon informed me he wrote a paper about my case, and the CT scans were going to be shown at the annual AMA meeting. My brain had stirred up great interest!

In the meantime Hank had his own traumatic time, added to his worries about me. He had his own work that often included some traveling. He looked after the stores, together with Kathy and Janie, who both worked there now. Late at night he still took care of the money left in the stores. Besides all that, he came to see me every single day that I spent in the hospital. During that time he drove forty-four hundred miles extra just to see me. He didn't eat right, and he became skinnier and skinnier. I worried more about him than about myself. It was tearing heartbreak to live apart that long. Janie came to see me often, and Kathy came with the kids on weekends. They were all a little dazed by what had happened to their mother and grandmother, who had always been so healthy.

I returned home the day before Easter that year, a shadow of my former self. I was so weak that it took me all morning to get dressed. I had to rest between each item of clothing. And of course, there were the three stores. After three weeks I tried to go to work half a day each day. The girls had done their very best, but it was time for me to take some of the work off their hands.

Through good fortune we were able to sell the children's store almost immediately. The buyers came to us and asked if we would sell it. One-third of the work disappeared, which proved to be a blessing.

At the hospital Hank and I had been told by my doctors that seizures of the brain would be unavoidable. They put me on anti-seizure medication, which did strange things to me. Often I forgot what I was talking about—it was as if there were "holes" in my thinking.

One morning at the breakfast table, Hank took my hand and seriously said, "I want you to quit that medication."

"But I can't," I nervously answered. "Just imagine that I might have a seizure, in the stores, or on the street!"

Hank was not about to let the subject go. He had made up his mind. "I am convinced that that stuff is not good for you. Besides, the Lord healed you, and He never does half a job. I want you to step out in faith."

He resumed eating. The case was settled—at least for him.

I still hesitated. Seizures terrified me. I knew in my heart, however, that Hank was right. I had been miraculously healed, and now it was up to me to prove my faith. We told the neurologist that I wanted to discontinue the medication. He disagreed, but said I could try it. I would have to wean myself slowly from the pills over a period of three weeks. He warned us that epilepsy could pop up five years later.

Looking back over the decades since, God indeed healed me completely and proved Hank right. My brain settled down nicely, working perfectly again. The extreme physical weakness lasted several more years, but that too eventually improved. Hank and I were able to pick up our lives again, and resumed our Sunday mornings in the hills.

The entire experience left me in awe. I kept thinking, why me? Why did the Lord heal me? I had never done anything for Him! He saved me throughout my life, especially during the war, and now He had healed me! And I kept asking, why me? I felt so humbled. What had I ever done for Him?

I asked Hank, "What can I do for the Lord? I want to do something back for Him."

Hank shook his head. "Sweetheart," he answered, "you can't do anything for the Lord. You can't pay Him back. He gives it all to you through grace. We cannot earn our way into heaven. It is His gift to us, because we believe in His Son Jesus Christ."

I pondered that in my heart but silently decided that if the time ever came that I could do something for the Lord, I hoped He would let me.

Nineteen

IN THE MID-1980s our family received two exquisite gifts in the form of two beautiful, tiny toddlers from Korea, adopted by Janie and David. Candy came first, followed by Shelby about 18 months later. The entire family was on hand when each of them arrived by plane from the Far East. We all promptly fell in love with our new family members, from the grandparents to the youngest cousin.

Love is a beautiful thing. There is always enough to go around. Each new child is loved exactly like the previous child. These little girls immediately became our own flesh and blood, and we thanked God for His great gift! Hardly an evening went by that Hank and I didn't visit our new grandchildren. Erik, Ian, and Becky loved to play with them, and it was a joy to see them all together.

It was because of these two lovely girls that Hank became a devoted churchgoer. Through all our ups and downs, and all the obvious evidence of the Lord working in our lives, helping and saving us, he still refused to give up his childhood conviction that religion found in churches was not anything he desired. He found God in the hills, and the trees, and the mountains and lakes. God's creation was Hank's place of worship, and being the stubborn fellow he was, nothing could shake him.

Candy and Shelby went to Sunday school and learned all kinds of cute songs. They loved to perform for us, and we, too, had to learn the songs and sing with them.

One day Candy asked, "Grandpa, why don't you go to church? Don't you like church?" Her big brown eyes looked at him intently. She waited for an answer.

Hank answered, a bit startled, "I don't know."

On the way home he grumbled, "Did you hear that? If even my grandchildren start talking about me going to church, maybe I should, just to show them."

I held my breath, not answering. Would he really go?

That same week Hank received a note from the church's music pastor, asking him if he would be willing to videotape the Easter concert. The pastor had heard from Kathy, who sang in the choir at that time, that her dad liked videotaping. Indeed that had become Hank's hobby. Hank decided he would look into it, and went to talk to the music pastor.

That Easter found us in church, with Hank videotaping an event for the very first time. He learned much, and became better and better at this new activity. For the following 18 years Hank could be found most Sundays on top of his perch, surrounded by his camera equipment, and enjoying every minute of it. When he was asked to join the men's Bible study group on Tuesday mornings, he accepted, and that time each week became very special to him.

For the first time since coming to the United States, we made some real friends and were soon part of a lively fellowship.

Our lives flowed on, sometimes hitting bumpy rocks, sometimes enjoying a time of peace. Hank retired from the company he had helped build up. It was rather a forced retirement. The company had been sold, and the new owner's ideas were very different from the way the previous owners had run the business. Hank was frustrated about seeing changes that he felt were detrimental to the company's welfare. We decided it would be better for him to draw back now.

At about that same time, Kathy and her second husband divorced. During this marriage Kathy had become diabetic due to extreme stress, according to her doctor. It had been the second intolerable marriage for her. She decided to fulfill a lifelong dream and become a nurse. With a PELL grant, a scholarship, and help from us, she was able to go to school.

Hank started driving a school bus for the local Christian school to help her out some more. It was a difficult time financially for Kathy, but she made ends meet, although barely. On top of all that Kathy, and also Hank and I, went through the tumultuous years of three teenagers.

During that time we sold our building downtown and combined two businesses into one. We had started with one store, and now were back to only one business, which lightened the load considerably. Not long after that, I retired from 23 years in the women's apparel business and heaved a sigh of relief. With all the malls cropping up, business had become stressful and difficult, and I was glad to get rid of the daily worries.

In the early 1990s Janie and David decided to move to the country and found five acres in a very quiet area. The house they built was the first one at their end of the country road. When we visited the big, empty field after they bought the land, I became worried.

"It is so isolated here," I complained. "You will be murdered in your beds!"

David and Janie thought that was so funny!

Looking back at that comment, I have to confess there was probably more danger on our city street than out there in the fresh country air. Our street had become completely packed with small tract houses, many of them used as rentals. We found unknown children in our yard from time to time, and were located on a street corner where a school bus stop was. The children would be waiting out there every morning, sometimes fighting and yelling. One early morning our doorbell rang, and there stood a cold, small girl asking for help and telling us that the kids were fighting so much she was afraid to stand there.

We had a very sweet neighbor next door, a widow. Her yard was fenced, but fences certainly didn't seem to stop unwanted visitors. One day, Hank was outside puttering around, and he noticed a young man in his early twenties walk into her back yard, unzip his trousers, and actually use her yard as a bathroom! Hank immediately went to the fence and told the man to get out of there. What happened next still seems unbelievable. The man came to the fence mumbling angry words, ripped a board off of the top, and hit Hank in the head with it! Hank ended up bruised and bloody, and we realized that our "safe" home wasn't so safe anymore. We were very shaken by that episode, and our family became worried about us and the way the neighborhood was deteriorating.

David and Janie went to talk to the county and discovered that they could get a temporary permit to place an extra home on their property. They invited us to move out there, away from our increasingly unsafe city street. So, one year later Hank and I moved out there too, into a roomy manufactured home situated on a corner of their five acres, close to tall trees and blackberry bushes. We had a lot of good laughs about my original comment of being "murdered in your beds!" By then more houses were being built on their road, but far apart from one another.

Hank and I approached our fiftieth wedding anniversary and were hoping for some good, fun years yet.

Hank would sometimes say, "I think you and I are going to be very old together."

"That's fine with me," I'd reply. "I want to be married to you at least thirty more years."

We were blessed with a unique marriage. After falling in love on that cold night during the Hunger Winter in World War II, we never fell out of love. Of course, we had our disagreements, sometimes quite heated ones, but they never mattered. Being very different, we learned to respect each other. For instance, Hank loved potato salad but hated mayonnaise. When I mentioned that I made the salad with sour cream, he was perfectly happy and loved every bite of it. Of course, I used mayonnaise, with a dab of sour cream, and he never knew the difference. I am sure he pulled tricks like that with me too. That is how we respected each other!

I learned very early in our marriage that I had married a stubborn fellow, but I eventually learned to cope with that.

He was the most unselfish person I ever met. He never wanted anything for himself. The children and I and then the grandchildren

always came first. One thing he was fascinated with was tinkering around
in a motor home, making them suit his needs. Over the years we owned
several different ones. He loved to take trips to Kansas and Missouri
to see the relatives. Driving across Montana or Wyoming, stopping at
some lonely spot to make coffee and eat lunch was one of his greatest
pleasures.

He was never boring. One of my many character flaws is that I am
easily bored, even with people. But in all the years we were married,
Hank never bored me. He was full of surprises. Being a complex human
being, he could react totally opposite from the way I expected. Life with
him was exciting.

He also had no sense of color. One day we were going out to a friend's
house. He came out of the bedroom, dressed for the evening. Earlier he
had bought a pair of pink pants for five dollars. That is what he would
do, find the best bargains. For me nothing was too expensive; he wanted
me to buy anything I wished. For himself, however, it had to be the
cheapest of the cheap. The pink pants were definitely not suitable for a
gentleman his age. With them he wore a pumpkin-colored shirt. The
combination was awful! I refused to let him leave the house like that.

"You can't go visit people in that outfit!" I said.

"Why not? I like it."

"Because you look ridiculous! Those colors are hideous together,
and besides, why did you ever buy pink pants?"

"They were only five dollars!"

He stalked out of the room, and hollered over his shoulder, "Then
I am not going!"

I waited.

Pretty soon he came back again, and had traded the pumpkin shirt
for a light blue one, but kept the pink pants on. We went out that
night.

We had a remarkable relationship. We simply could not do without
each other. When he was gone, I would sit before the window watching
the road to see if he was coming back yet. He did the same. When we
were invited out to dinner, we were disappointed if we could not sit
next to each other. We talked together about any subject and made each

other laugh. We communicated constantly. We were best friends, totally in tune with each other.

The marriage never became stale, was always alive, and we could not imagine life without each other. We were convinced that God would keep us together until a ripe old age, and then we would die at the same time.

For a bossy, cocky guy, he was greatly dependent upon me. There were moments that I prayed to the Lord, "Please, Lord, when our time comes, let Hank die before me, because I don't want him to suffer the loss. He won't be able to handle it." I knew him so well and was convinced that he could not easily go on without me.

Often, after breakfast he would ask, "What do you want to do today?"

It was never about what he wanted to do; my wish was the most important.

Our favorite pastime was to take the motor home, drive to Rasar Park, find our favorite spot, and park for the day. Hank would fry hamburgers, I would unpack the rest of the goodies, and that was our special idea of heaven.

Our life together had never been more peaceful and tranquil. Kathy had finally found the love of her life in Mike, a splendid man for her. We loved him right away, as we had always loved Janie's David.

Becky was making a success of a career in the Air Force. The boys had outgrown their escapades and settled down. The younger girls were smart and doing well in school.

We loved our home and living close to Janie and David, and we were convinced that a long and happy life was still stretching out before us. We loved talking about our lives in the "olden days" back in Holland, where each of us had grown up so differently, and how the war had brought us together, but had also formed us and affected us.

I sometimes wanted to go back on a trip and see all the old places again. Hank refused.

"You can never go back," he told me many times. "Forget it. Our life is here, and what do you think you are going to find there?"

Even so, I sometimes thought how nice it would be to walk along the canals in Amsterdam, or see the old neighborhoods in Rotterdam, and the white sandy beaches of the North Sea. I didn't want to make a big issue of it, so I forgot about it. Maybe some day he would change his mind.

We were enjoying our "golden years" and told each other often how very blessed we were. We were involved in a wonderful church and were part of a great circle of friends. All our kids were doing well, and we loved our home. What more could anyone want?

Shortly after Hank's seventy-sixth birthday we learned he had cancer.

Twenty

DURING A ROUTINE colonoscopy, the tiny camera found a very ugly spot. The doctor was convinced it was colon cancer. He told us Hank needed immediate surgery, and the necessary preparations were set into motion.

Early the next morning, they wheeled Hank into the operating room from which he didn't emerge for many hours. I sat in the waiting room, inwardly shaking, with a constantly pounding heart. My Hank, that husky, healthy man, never sick a day in his life, so strong even in his seventies, was being operated on for cancer!

What a bad dream enveloped us now! I could hardly comprehend that such a thing could happen to us, Hank and Christina. Things were going so well, we loved our golden years together.

The oncologist, a marvelous doctor, told us Hank would have to undergo chemotherapy—18 treatments, each one three weeks apart. Hank balked at that. He would not do that! He had lost twelve inches out of his colon, and that should be enough. Kathy, our family nurse, talked him into accepting the chemo, and she was rather stern about it. I didn't really know what to say, and felt it was entirely up to Hank.

So the chemo treatments started. As predicted, they made him ill, although not nauseous. Modern drugs took care of that. It was the worst time. I accompanied him at first. I watched as he sat in a recliner with tubes going into his arm. It was hard to see my husband tied down in that chair with the poison entering his body. He did not want me to stay and finally told me firmly that I had to leave. I cried on the way out of the hospital.

One morning, after he had undergone several treatments, I heard him talking on the phone. He wanted to talk to his oncologist. I wondered what he was up to. I heard him informing the doctor that he would not be back for further treatments. I sat down with a smack on the nearest chair.

After a short conversation, Hank hung up the phone and nodded with great satisfaction.

"What on earth was that all about?" I wanted to know.

"I am not going on with those chemo treatments. They are making me sick and weak, and I don't feel like it." He stuck out his chin, and I knew he meant business.

Then he said, "I told the doctor that I was through, and that I would take my chances with the Lord. If He wants to heal me, He will."

I was curious. "And what did the doctor answer?"

"He is a very wise man," my husband declared. "He said he never argues with a patient."

Thus ended Hank's chemo treatments. He received only four out of the 18.

During follow-up exams and CT scans, no trace of cancer was found.

We had weathered this scary episode very well, and we settled down to our pleasant life once again.

Exactly one year later Hank fell off a ladder while working in the barn and broke his upper arm. He had landed on the side of his face, and he was black-and-blue. His broken arm rested in a sling for six weeks, and he was frustrated and angry. He insisted that he could still drive, and so he did. But I had to help him shower and dress, and for the independent guy he was, that made him feel humiliated. Finally that episode ended too, and we both were sure our troubles had come to an end.

Once again we took a motor home trip to Kansas and Missouri, enjoying it more than ever before.

Hank celebrated his 80th birthday in January 2004 with an open house for friends and a family party afterwards. He had been declared totally free from cancer just a few weeks before, so it was a double celebration. He loved to be 80, he told friends. It was a dignified age.

That summer he slowed down. He always loved being busy, especially in his barn. He fussed with this and that, making things like benches, a picnic table, even a lean-to at the back of the property. Often he came inside, complaining that he didn't know why he was so tired. His long days were getting shorter and shorter, and he looked a little pale. I told him he was no spring chicken any longer and at 80 it was normal to be tired. He liked to be busy, but perhaps it was time to slow down a bit.

When I told him that, he scowled at me. A vague, uneasy feeling took possession of me. He started eating less, which was another point of worry for me. Finally, that fall I talked him into a physical checkup. Instead of refusing, he went to see his doctor, and that really scared me. I had expected a very loud and determined "No!"

Our family doctor found a large lump in Hank's neck and sent him to a surgeon for a biopsy. We were told Hank had non-Hodgkin's lymphoma, malignant tumors of the lymph system. Further testing showed it was a very aggressive kind.

We went back to the oncologist, and this time it became clear to everyone that Hank had to undergo chemo treatments. He had no other choice. Without any arguments from him, he went back on chemo. The treatments sapped his strength, although he tried to live as normal a life as possible. He still drove our motor home to our favorite spots for our hamburger cookouts, and he continued to do little projects around the place.

Life now revolved around Hank's treatments. He finished one series, and our hopes were high. We just knew they had worked. Another CT scan told us differently, and after some hesitation from the doctors due to his age, he was given a series of much stronger intravenous medications.

During all these months he still did the videotaping of the Sunday morning services at church, and he never missed the men's Bible study on Tuesday morning. He always scheduled his treatments after the Bible studies that day.

I lived with a deep fear during all that time. I wondered if Hank would die and I would be left alone without him.

A third series of ever stronger treatments did not bring about any improvement, either. The disease seemed unstoppable, and the many tumors kept growing and multiplying. There was one more treatment left, the final option. We were sent to the Fred Hutchinson Cancer Center in Seattle. Janie drove us, because by then Hank was becoming very weak. We were told about a nuclear infusion that might help, and it would be done at the University of Washington Medical Center.

The two treatments, a few days apart, took place in October. Hank would be radioactive after them, and I was told I would have to keep my distance from him. Keep my distance from my sick husband? *No way*, I thought. He needed me more than ever.

In December we knew that the final option had not worked. There was nothing left to do. Back in the doctor's office, when told of the final prognosis, Hank asked, "Am I going to die now?"

The doctor's face turned red. He was a sweet, sensitive man. He did not answer.

But Hank had to know. "How much time have I got?" he asked.

The answer came. "If we talk of years, or months, I would say months. And if it would be between many months, or a few, I would say a few months."

It was deadly still in the small room.

Hank stirred, and then calmly said, "I am going to die then."

I saw the doctor could not answer. All he managed to say was that he would like to see Hank in January. So it was decided.

Kathy was with us in the doctor's office. After leaving the clinic, we decided to go to Kathy's house, where she called Janie right away. Janie came quickly, and the four of us sat around in Kathy's living room, not saying much. What could one say? When Hank and I finally returned to our home, we did not talk much. He was still very sick from those nuclear infusions. They had destroyed his stomach, and he hardly ate any more.

No matter what I cooked for him, his most favorite soups and puddings, he could hardly eat. He became thinner and thinner. A very bad thing that occurred was that he quit communicating with me. He rarely spoke, or smiled, and I felt I had already lost him.

At Christmas our family knew that it would be Hank's last. Becky came home on leave from the Air Force to be with her beloved Grandfather, and brought little Hank, her little boy. The two Hanks met each other for the first time.

Hank had his 82nd birthday in January, and we again knew it would be his last. The entire family gathered again, without Becky this time because she had to return to the air base in Texas. Hank sat in his big recliner, dressed in his favorite red plaid shirt, and we all gathered around him. We ate pizza from plates on our laps, and even Hank tried to eat a tiny piece. His conversation was quite animated that night, telling stories from his youth during World War II, and of course, talking about his favorite subject, the Lord Jesus Christ.

He told the children and grandchildren to give themselves to Christ, because there was no other way of living. He was the old Hank. It was a very good evening, and for a little while it seemed impossible that he would be gone soon.

Hank's final appointment with his oncologist did not last very long. Hospice would take over now. A hospital bed was put in our family room next to the windows, and the hospice people started to come around, a male nurse, a social worker, and a female chaplain. They all were super, wonderful people.

Hank no longer wanted visitors. He did see our pastor, however. Pastor Kent came to visit one afternoon, and Hank told him that he had seen heaven. The way he told it, he had suddenly seen a great light, and felt such love as he had never experienced before. He did not hear any music or voices and had not seen anyone specific, but the love was so enormous that he didn't want to come back. He thought he was in heaven at last. Then he noticed the television set, and he saw other familiar things, and he knew he was still alive. He was deeply disappointed, he told the pastor.

I was stunned.

"You never told me that." I felt tears in my eyes.

Had our separation become so true that Hank would not tell me something that deeply spiritual?

"What do you think it means?" he asked the pastor.

Kent hesitated. Then he answered, "I don't know much about those things, but I am sure of one thing. That was God's gift to you."

Hank smiled weakly and closed his eyes.

Besides knowing that our life together would soon be over, and grieving over that, my deepest distress was over the fact that Hank did not seem to want to talk to me. I had total care of him, day and night. Most nights I slept in my chair next to his bed. In the morning, after my shower, I would come by his bedside and say, "Hello there, good morning! The night nurse has left and here is your day nurse. This is the one who flirts with you and kisses you."

I could not even get a feeble smile from him. I thought I understood. He was in great pain and discomfort, and how could he talk to me when he was that miserable? But one day he suddenly looked me full in the eyes and said, "I can't look at you, because I am going to cry if I do."

Then I understood. He had always taken care of me, totally. He was my protector, my husband, my friend, and now he knew I would be left behind, without him. The thought that I would be alone, without him to watch over me and take care of me, was torturing him. I turned my back, because I did not want him to see my tears.

By the time February arrived, Hank was on morphine, without restrictions. The pain had become excruciating. He stopped eating or drinking, and we all knew the end was near. He had diminished to a skeleton, and the Hank I had known all my life was already gone.

In the early hours of February 6, 2006, I knew that this would be Hank's last night on earth. I felt an unreal calm. He was home, among his familiar things, and surrounded by loving family. We were still a team.

An eerie stillness hung in the softly lit room. I could not hear even the labored sound of breathing. I bent over him. His chest moved slowly, his eyes were tightly closed. With a feathery touch I stroked his hollow, sunken cheek. Then I lowered myself carefully onto the chair beside the bed.

For the first time in my life I was in the presence of a dying human being, and he was the love of my life, my soul mate. His beautiful, broad, and enormously strong hands, which could also express great tenderness, had become thin, fleshless, and amazingly small. They tightly gripped the sheet that he had pulled up to his chin. The strong, muscular body, ravaged by the ugly, destructive cancer, had dwindled to almost nothing, barely lifting the blankets. I pictured his face as it used to be—without a blemish, with splendid color, tanned from a life outdoors, bright green eyes with a perpetual twinkle, and a lovely deep dimple in his chin. Now his eyes no longer twinkled, his cheeks receded over sharp bones, and the healthy tan was transformed into a sickly greenish color.

I was just slipping into sleep when he stirred and moaned, instantly alerting me. His withered lips looked dry and chapped. According to the nurse's instructions I squirted a few drops of morphine into his mouth. Mechanically he tried to swallow, after which he became quiet again.

Scrambled thoughts flitted through my mind. We would never experience the joy of our sixtieth anniversary, only two months away. With Hank's life gone, mine would stop too. How could I continue living?

I touched his forehead, his arms. He felt cold. He shivered from cold lately, a man who had always felt too warm. I pulled an extra blanket over his body and tenderly tucked it in, snug all around him.

In the recliner behind me Candy stirred, changing her position. She had insisted on staying with me this night. I preferred to be alone, but recognizing her loving and willing heart, had gracefully accepted. I pulled her blanket around her shoulders too, and settled down once more, keeping my eyes fixed on the dear face of the man I loved.

His chest was still slowly moving up and down. I felt a strange quiet around us, as if the whole world was holding its breath. Finally I dozed, in spite of my uncomfortable chair.

A loud, gurgling sound startled me. I jumped up, while two loud cries tore through the room. The head on the pillow slumped aside. Panicked, I put my hand on his chest. Nothing, it no longer moved. The body was completely still. I stood there, staring with unbelieving eyes, deep silence surrounding me. Hank's soul had left him, lifting him into the heaven he so strongly believed in. Death had now finished this long and productive life, so totally devoted to God, his wife, and his family. The terrible suffering had ended. There would be no more pain and tears for him—he had entered into a new existence in a new life.

Candy was still sleeping undisturbed. I slowly sank onto my chair, keeping my eyes on the man who had been and always would be the love of my life, my best friend, and lifelong companion. It was all finished. Something indefinable had left him; he didn't look like a living person any longer. His true self had departed, leaving behind an empty shell.

It is said, when a man is drowning, he sees his entire life unfolding before him. I was drowning, in a life gone forever, and I saw how it all began . . . .

Hank and I met when I was eight and he was nine. We stood there, staring at each other, not saying one word . . . .

Picking Up the Pieces...

THE STORY OF Hank and I began 76 years ago, when we first met as children. Only I remain now. I have told you this story about two simple people, caught up in a war and the aftermath, leaving their homeland and starting a new life across an ocean, because I felt it necessary.

After Hank's death I was devastated. I felt lonely and utterly miserable. He no longer came in from the outdoors with rosy cheeks, smelling like fresh air and stamping his feet on the doormat, hollering, "Is the coffee ready?"

I knew deep in my heart that he would not want me to become a crybaby. So often I had heard him say, after some disaster befell us, "Let's just pick up the pieces, and go on."

So that is what I have decided to do, pick up the pieces and start counting my blessings. There are many. Above all there is my family— two marvelous daughters, five grandchildren, several in-laws, and even a bunch of great-grandchildren. I adore my church and all the people who have shown me such love and kindness, and above all I am intensely aware of the love and comfort from the Lord. The blessing list keeps growing. I have learned that life is a great gift and we must make the most of it.

A year after Hank died, I traveled to Holland to go on a bus tour. I had always wanted to go back, but Hank didn't want to. I fully expected to find the old neighborhoods and to walk along the canals of Amsterdam, revisiting the places where Hank and I had walked, and kissed.

I was disappointed to discover that the changes were enormous. Rotterdam and Amsterdam have become giant cities, crowded, dirty, and unbelievably immoral. I remembered Hank's words, "You can't go back. Only look ahead." I felt foreign in my homeland, a stranger without any connection to a past. I had become a true American, and felt proud of it. The only places I enjoyed were in the countryside. I had rarely left the city of my youth so had few memories of the country, and there we still passed through picture pretty places. The trip proved one important truth to me: I could do things on my own.

These last few years I have rediscovered myself. I have enjoyed the freedom to go where I want to go when I want to do it, but with the loss of my soul mate forever in the back of my mind. I know he lives on; we have been parted only for a brief time. I will see him again. And until that glorious day arrives, I will do my best to live each day honoring his memory, and giving all the thanks and glory to the One who brought us together.

LaVergne, TN USA
03 February 2010

171985LV00003B/201/P